WEREWOLVES

Other titles sure to chill and thrill you:

WEREWOLVES

NANCY GARDEN

J. B. LIPPINCOTT COMPANY/Philadelphia and New York

j
398.469

U.S. Library of Congress Cataloging in Publication Data

Garden, Nancy.
  Werewolves.

  (The Weird and horrible library)
  SUMMARY: Examines the origins of werewolf legends, the characteristics of
these beasts, and records of their existence throughout history.
  Bibliography: p.
  1. Werwolves—Juvenile literature. [1. Werewolves] I. Title.
GR830.W4G37   398.2'454   72–13280
ISBN–0–397–31463–9   ISBN–0–397–31464–7 (pbk.)

TO MY GOOD FRIENDS

DICKIE, LIBBY, AND DONNY WHEELER

ACKNOWLEDGMENTS

Pictures appearing on pages 21, 24, 25, 27, 32, 33, 43, 48, 54, 58, 63, 77, 80, 83, 102, 104, 109, 113, 115 courtesy of New York Public Library Picture Collection; page 98 from IN SEARCH OF DRACULA, by McNally and Florescu (New York Graphic Society, Ltd.), permission Kunstmuseum, Vienna; pages 39, 51, 68, 120 published by permission of University Books, Inc., Secaucus, New Jersey; page 14 courtesy Culver Pictures.

CONTENTS

INTRODUCTION

WEREWOLVES—who hasn't paled at the thought of them when walking a long, lonely road at night? The moon rides high above the treetops, clouds scudding across its face. The wind scrapes branches back and forth against each other, cracking, creaking. An owl swoops down on an unsuspecting mouse, whose terror-stricken shriek is lost in a whir of heavy wings. A cloud hides the fading moon; the road leads up a hill, around a bend, and into a thicker patch of woods. Suddenly . . .

The rest of that story depends on the teller: peasant wife, recently freed slave, traveling priest, young father of a strangely marked baby. The werewolf stories of these and other people will be told in the following pages. Some of the stories may surprise you a little, especially if your knowledge about werewolves comes primarily from the movies. Werewolves, of course, were not invented by moviemakers. They are creatures from folklore, characters in tales told long before the days of movies and television. Like most legends, werewolf stories are a mixture of fact and fantasy, history and fiction. Hollywood werewolves are often quite different from their folklore ancestors. For example, in the movies, people who are werewolves get fierce and hairy when the moon is full, but they usually do not change into bona fide four-legged wolves. Most real werewolves, however, do. Their hands and feet change to paws, their arms to legs; their noses grow long and their ears become pointed and move to the tops of their heads. Their teeth lengthen and their mouths change shape from human to canine. At last, their human voices vanish, and they are left with long-drawn wolf howls as their only means of expression. Only their eyes, with a glimmer of knowledge and intelligence, remain human.

Movie werewolves must usually be killed by silver bullets; most folklore werewolves can be killed like any other animal. You wouldn't get very far trying to defend yourself against a folklore werewolf with a silver candlestick unless you managed to hit him hard enough on the head to knock him out. But many Hollywood werewolves are so afraid of anything silver that they won't come near you if you simply hold a silver object up in front of them.

Becoming a werewolf is both easy and accidental according to the movies. All it usually takes is a nonfatal bite from someone who is a werewolf himself. But in folklore, becoming a werewolf was far more complicated.

Many people came to werewolfery because of arrangements with the Devil. Sometimes they were witches, pledged to worship the Devil and do his bidding. The Devil ordered such people to run through forest and village as wolves, terrorizing good churchgoing villagers. Or he told them to kill people and bring him their insides as a ritual sacrifice. Other werewolves were forced into pacts with the Devil, often in return for some kind of needed protection. The Devil would promise, for example, to guard a shepherd's flock—if the shepherd would agree to show a bored or shy person how to change himself into an exciting, fierce wolf in return for similar favors, or in return for the person's soul. Some of these Devil-made werewolves were glad to be able to turn into animals. Others were not, and were miserably unhappy till they were freed from what they considered a horrible curse. Folk legends don't say much about how the werewolves felt about all this—but in Hollywood movies the werewolf's unhappiness is usually a major theme.

Although there were also many werewolves in folklore who had little or nothing to do with the Devil, religious authorities, especially the Catholic Church in the Middle Ages, considered them all to be the Devil's servants. Many werewolves (or suspected werewolves) were burned at the stake as witches. Since witches worshiped the Devil instead of God, they were considered enemies of the Church. The cross and other religious objects were therefore often used by Church authorities to protect people and places against were-wolves.

Despite these folk traditions, movie and TV werewolves are rarely Devil-dealers. *The Wolf Man* (1941), probably the best known werewolf movie, is about a college student who turns into a werewolf in the usual Hollywood way: he gets bitten by one. That, as we've seen, isn't how folklore werewolves are made—but inter-estingly enough, it is how folklore vampires are made. It is as if Hollywood borrowed from vampire legends to embellish their own werewolf stories.

Actually, although there are many differences between the two creatures, there are also many similarities. The werewolf, of course, is a living person who has the ability to shift his shape into that of a wolf. The vampire, on the other hand, is an "undead" person—one suspended halfway between life and death—who can shapeshift at will but whose main occupation is drinking the blood of the living. According to many legends, werewolves become vampires after death. And, although their methods of attack differ, both creatures more often than not aim for the same part of their victims' anatomy: the jugular vein in the throat. Vampires are usually portrayed as being the more intelligent of the two—but they frequently have a

Lon Chaney as Lawrence Talbot, The Wolf Man, in a Hollywood version of a werewolf victim. The movies borrowed from the legends and terrified audiences, but often the information in them was inaccurate.

special regard for wolves (or for werewolves), either keeping them as pets or commanding packs. And, perhaps recognizing the terror that wolves inspire, vampires sometimes choose wolf-shape as one of their many disguises.

Since there are so many connections between the two creatures, it is not surprising that vampires and werewolves frequently appear together in movies. There's *The House of Frankenstein* (1944), for example, in which Lawrence Talbot (the Wolf Man) encounters both Dracula, the most famous vampire of all time, and Frankenstein's notorious monster. There's also *The House of Dracula* (1945) and *Abbott and Costello Meet Frankenstein* (1948) in which Dracula and the Wolf Man appear together again. And then, of course, there was the recent TV series *Dark Shadows* in which a vampire and a werewolf had various adventures as members of the same family in a small town in Maine.

Certainly the movies and TV have done their best to make both vampires and werewolves pleasingly horrifying and eerie. Cleverly executed special effects, carefully applied makeup (the Wolf Man's took five hours to put on), and skillful acting and directing have all contributed to the terror werewolves and their fellow creatures can arouse. There always seems to be an audience for this kind of thing; people always seem to enjoy being scared if there's no real danger. Perhaps being scared in this way provides an escape from the humdrum day-to-day world; perhaps people enjoy imagining themselves the heroes or victims in horror movies. In any case, it's not a bit dangerous to sit safely in one's living room or in one's movie-theater seat and watch Lon Chaney, Jr., as Lawrence Talbot, the Wolf Man, change slowly from a man to a ghastly wolflike creature. But if a person saw a man in real life grow slowly hairy and beastlike till he was scarcely recognizable as a human being, he'd no doubt be too overcome by terror to enjoy the excitement of the experience. The peasants of Transylvania, the shepherds of ancient Greece, the townspeople of Europe in the Middle Ages had no need of movies and TV to turn their hearts to slush and their knees to jelly. When a friend plucked a man by the sleeve centuries ago in the marketplace and said in a horrified whisper, "My neighbor's child was killed by a wolf last night—a *were*wolf!" there was no way the man could tell himself "It's only a story." In those days, in the minds of most people anyway, *it was always the real thing.*

Several people have helped me put this book together, and I would like to thank them: the staff of the Boston Athenaeum; Joel Lamon, who gave me information about the rare disease porphyria; Diana Miller, who told me about the disease in the first place—and the late Montague Summers, whose book *The Werewolf*, published in the United States by University Books, Inc., was a never-ending fund of information.

NANCY GARDEN, 1972

WEREWOLVES

1

WHAT IS A WEREWOLF?

ONE PLEASANT SUMMER DAY in the late 1500's, a French boy, Benedict Bidel, and his younger sister were out walking. The mountain air was fresh and life seemed pretty good to them—perhaps it was a holiday or maybe it was late afternoon and, their chores done, they were strolling home. In any case, when they came to a tree heavy with fruit, Benedict told his sister to wait while he climbed up to pick some; it looked too good to resist. Imagine how his heart sank when, from his perch high in the tree, he heard his sister's bloodcurdling scream! Imagine his panic when he saw a huge tailless wolf about to attack her!

Benedict dropped the fruit he had picked and scrambled down the tree. Bravely, he pushed his sister aside and faced the wolf himself. Some versions of the story say the wolf mauled Benedict with long, sharp claws. Others say the wolf had hands instead of paws and that it pulled a knife on him. Still other accounts say the wolf grabbed Benedict's knife and plunged it deep into the boy's throat. All agreed that someone—a neighbor, a group of peasants—ran to Benedict's rescue and beat the wolf off. Unfortunately, help came too late. Benedict was horribly hurt and in a day or so he died.

Before he died, though, Benedict reported that the wolf's paws looked like human hands.

"We're not looking for a wild wolf, then," the neighbors realized. They added in horrified whispers: "We're looking for a werewolf!"

They found one, too. There in the bushes, not far from where Benedict had been mauled, the neighbors found the body of a young woman, Perrenette Gandillon. She was dead and couldn't speak in her defense, but some of the people said they remembered seeing her walking on all fours once or twice. "An odd one," they agreed, and some said, "She was a witch."

You would think the story would end there, with Perrenette's death. It doesn't. Time and many retellings have mixed up the details—this was, after all, around four hundred years ago—but apparently it wasn't long before Perrenette's brother Pierre was accused of being a werewolf, too. Then Pierre's son, Georges, was accused, and then his sister, Antoinette. There was a trial, under Henri Bouget, a judge who was well-known for sentencing many a sixteenth-century witch. Bouget said that Pierre and Georges no longer looked human, and had thickly matted hair and filthy, clawlike nails. He believed that, in wolf-shape, they attended sabbats (meetings of witches) where they worshiped the Devil. Antoinette, it was said, confessed to making hail, which in those days was a sure sign of witchcraft. All three, like many werewolves before and after, were burned at the stake.

No one will ever know what really happened that summer day to Benedict and his sister. They might have been attacked by a real wolf that had already killed Perrenette; the neighbors, finding Perrenette's body and knowing her to be strange, could simply have put the evidence together incorrectly. Or, if Perrenette was the attacker, Benedict and his rescuers could have said "she looked like a wolf" instead of "she was a wolf." No one will ever know if Perren-

An English werewolf drawing from a sixteenth-century French manuscript.

ette and her family really practiced witchcraft or worshiped the Devil, or whether they could change themselves into wolves. All anyone really knows is that back in the 1500's many people firmly believed that such things were possible—that Perrenette and many other people truly were werewolves.

The word werewolf means "man-wolf" and is most commonly used to describe a person who can change himself (or herself) into a wolf or some other animal. (The word *lycanthrope* is also often used for this, although it has another meaning, too: a person with a mental disorder which makes him *think* he is a wolf.) In Africa, the animal chosen is likely to be a leopard or hyena; in Asia, a tiger; in the United States, a coyote or a buffalo. In almost all cases, the animal has these characteristics:

1. It is commonly found in the area
2. It is feared by the inhabitants
3. It has been known to attack people and farm animals

All these characteristics have fit wolves at various times and in various places. Before man covered much of his living space with cities and towns there were wolves in almost all parts of the world: Europe, North America, South America, parts of Asia; there were wolflike creatures in Africa and on the island of Tasmania off Australia.

In Ireland, there were so many wolves that Englishmen referred to it as "The Wolf Land" till the late 1700's. The Irish wolfhound was specially bred to hunt them, as was the Russian wolfhound in Russia. According to folklore, there were good wolves in Ireland as well as bad. One saint, St. Ronan, was said to have had a gentle wolf for a pet and another, St. Molva, held a yearly festival honoring wolves. People in ancient Ireland carried a wolf's tooth for luck, much as people elsewhere have carried a rabbit's foot. But by and large, wolves were not considered good—and werewolves were considered worse. St. Patrick himself is said to have put a curse on one Irish family which forced them to turn into wolves periodically—thus making them werewolves.

Although there are many different kinds of wolves, ranging in size from large to small and in color from red to black, the kind that commonly appears in werewolf stories is large and gray. It is an unusually strong animal, primarily a stealthy night-hunter, although it is sometimes seen during the day. Its eerie long-drawn howl sends shivers up and down the bravest of spines and its yellowish eyes, glowing red when they catch light at night, have frightened many an ordinarily brave traveler.

Another thing that makes wolves frightening is their habit of hunting in packs. It is one thing to be faced with one wild animal on a lonely forest road; it is quite another to be faced with a howling mob. Even gentle animals like cows are frightening when large numbers of them stampede.

Wolves, despite all stories to the contrary, do not often attack man. But a hungry wolf will eat any kind of meat he can find. As people settled in remote parts of the world, they moved into the wolves' territory, frightening off creatures the wolves fed upon and becoming handy prey themselves. Even nowadays, wolves frequently run out of food in winter when some of their animal victims hibernate and others die for lack of grass and leaves to eat. In the winter of 1875, some 160 people, it was estimated, were attacked by starving wolves in Russia. A couple of years before that, the wolves had destroyed hundreds of cattle. A hungry wolf who knows his way to a village where he has found fat cows will probably return when

(Overleaf) An 1868 engraving of wolves attacking a buffalo herd.

he is hungry again. If the cows aren't available, he'll take what is—a wounded bird, a goat, a helpless baby.

The fact that wolves rarely attack man, except when they are extremely hungry, doesn't make them any the less terrifying when they do attack. Nor does the fact that, especially as individuals, wolves *can* be gentle. Wolves have been tamed and kept as pets. Some have even proved to be as loyal as their domesticated descendants, dogs. Wolves are loyal among themselves, too, for they often mate for life and stay together in family groups, with both parents caring for the cubs. It was a she-wolf who suckled Remus and his twin brother Romulus, founder of Rome. Rudyard Kipling, in his *Jungle Book*, tells the story of an Indian boy, Mowgli, who was brought up by wolves and considered them his brothers. Mowgli's story isn't true but it is based on truth for, especially in India, there have been many well-documented reports of small children being suckled and cared for by wolves. Some of these children, in fact, got so used to living and eating as wolves that they died when given human care and food.

Even so, there aren't many people who wouldn't be terrified by the sight and sound of a pack of hungry wolves swooping down on their prey, be it a couple of rabbits, a herd of sheep, or a group of peace-loving country villagers. In many parts of the world, wolves were the most—or the only—frightening animals around, so they were also the most hated and the most talked-about. Even back in biblical times, wolves were hated so much they were used as symbols of evil. Anything which destroyed people's means of livelihood would, of course, have been considered bad, but wolves, since they were so frightening and since their main victims—sheep—were so gentle, seemed especially evil.

In some countries, a wolf's head nailed to the front door was believed to be powerful protection against witchcraft—almost as if the wolf, creature of evil, could not be molested by evil beings and in

A wolf pack attacking sheep.

that negative way, at least, could do good. Pliny, a Roman writer who lived in the first century A.D., reported that a certain hair in a wolf's tail was believed to be a strong love charm. According to American Indian belief, a wolfskin tom-tom was more powerful than one made of sheepskin. An ancient Norse saga tells of a boy

who was a coward till he ate a wolf's heart; then he became out-
standingly brave. Elsewhere, it was believed that wolf meat cured
melancholy and colic.

People drew comparisons between men and wolves, which is not
as farfetched as it seems if you remember Mowgli, Romulus and
Remus, and other wolf-children. A wild animal that can feed and
take care of human children—especially one which, unlike many
other animals, forms "families" of its own—does seem to have
human characteristics. Expressions like "He's a lone wolf," "wolf
whistle," "hungry as a wolf," and "wolf in sheep's clothing" bear
this out also. Wolves and other animals which appear in were-beast
stories have another very important human characteristic: they can
be both good and bad, gentle and fierce, kind and cruel. The strange
ability of folklore's special invention, the werewolf, to shift shape
from that of a "good" man to that of an "evil" wolf expresses the
same conflict between good and evil that people have always strug-
gled with in themselves.

II

SHAPESHIFTING

SHAPESHIFTING is an idea that has fascinated man almost since he first became aware of sharing his surroundings with creatures other than himself. Primitive man lived much more closely with animals than modern man; he often took them, quite literally, to be his brothers.

In some tribes, people believed that they shared their souls with a certain animal. An African tribesman, for example, might believe that he and a leopard were one, while an Eskimo's soul brother might be a bear, and an American Indian's a buffalo. Many American Indians believed their ancestors were animals, so certain animals were sacred to certain tribes. The Osages, for example, believed they came from a snail who turned into a human man and married a girl who became a beaver; they had great respect for both snails and beavers. Another tribe felt the same way about dogs. An Indian, according to their legend, once had a dog who gave birth to eight puppies. Whenever he went out, he would tie them up—and whenever he approached the tent on his way home, he would hear what sounded like children giggling and talking. When he went inside, though, there were the puppies, tied up as he had left them.

One day he only pretended to go out, and when he sneaked up on his "puppies" he saw children instead, with puppy-skins lying nearby. He burned the skins, and the children stayed in human form and grew up to found a new tribe.

Many people have believed that men become animals after death. Some American Indians believed that a person killed by an animal would then turn into that animal. On an island off the Ivory Coast in Africa, and in the Pacific island group called Tonga, people believed that certain large bats were the souls of dead people. Butterflies, in one part of Ireland, were thought to be the souls of grandfathers. Navajo Indians believed that evil men, in punishment for their sins, were turned into coyotes after death.

To the Hindus of India, animals and men are very closely related for they develop from each other in a long chain stretching from the most humble to the most noble. An individual might start life as a lowly worm, for example, and then, after death, live again as an insect. Later, he might reappear as a fish, then a frog, then maybe a bird, then a small animal, then a larger one, and finally, after many changes, a man. He will then be reborn over and over again, each time into a somewhat "higher" position (some animal positions are higher than some human positions). If he lives one of his lives evilly, he must drop a step on the scale till he has made up for his misdeeds. Reincarnation—implying belief in this kinship among all creatures—shows that shapeshifting may not be as strange and fantastic as it sounds.

Other beliefs and practices contributed to the development of werewolf legends. Imagine this scene: You are a small child, a member of a primitive tribe in ancient times. It has been a bad winter. The hunters of your tribe haven't killed any game for weeks. Undaunted, they are again going into the forest to hunt—but this time, before they go, they are going to make sure they don't come back empty-handed. The night before, dressed in the skins of the deer they hope to kill, they dance around a blazing campfire. You don't know any of this, though; you are only a small child and no one discusses tribal business with you. Perhaps, on the night of the deer-dance, you wake up and peer out of your hut. What do you see? Deer, leaping and prancing in the flickering light! While you watch, fascinated, some of the hunters leave the circle and shed their deer-skins. Suddenly they leap back into the light—men now, no longer deer. What do you think, small-child-to-whom-no-one-explains-things? Probably that these are deer who have changed into men—or men who have changed into deer and back again.

The practice of dressing in skins and pretending to be a certain kind of animal was a popular hunting technique among ancient tribal peoples. Ceremonial dances in skins were believed to lure the animal to the hunting ground, or to encourage that particular species to multiply. Sometimes, too, hunters wore wild-animal skins while they were actually hunting in order to disguise themselves. Dressed as buffalo, American Indians were able to pass freely through a herd and eventually lead the choicest buffalo into a trap. Eskimos found they could get closer to seals if they wore sealskins and barked the way seals do. Again, someone who didn't understand this technique could easily think that these hunters had turned into the animals they were impersonating.

People have dressed as animals for other reasons, too. In Scandinavia, Norsemen dressed in bearskins in order to frighten their enemies. Cherokee Indians, when forced to travel alone in winter, imitated animals that were not bothered by the cold in the hope that they, too, would be able to keep warm. People in other parts of the

(Overleaf) Undoubtedly, some were-animal legends grew from Indian ceremonies like this one.

world had human scapegoats. (A scapegoat is an animal, usually a goat, onto which primitive peoples believed they could transfer their sins or bad luck.) In ancient Tibet, a person was chosen periodically to act as scapegoat—and, dressed in an animal skin, he would be driven into the wilderness.

People long ago who impersonated animals, for whatever reason, may have felt that they were really transformed into the animals they pretended to be. Perhaps this is because of the intense concentration it takes to appear to be something one is not—as anyone who is good at acting or at pretending will understand.

Certainly many werewolves have been insistent in their belief that they really had turned into wolves—sometimes with tragic results. In Italy in the 1540's there was a man who could not control his wolflike cravings. He murdered several people, biting them as a wolf would. When he was caught, even though he looked like a normal man, he insisted he was a wolf. "Then where is your fur?" asked his captors. "It grows on the inside," he told them. Unfortunately, they tried to prove him wrong by cutting into his flesh, and he died of his wounds.

The traditional werewolf in folklore, however, had his fur on the outside. He shifted his shape periodically to that of a wolf either because he wanted to or because he was made to. While in wolf-shape, he attacked animals or people, often killing and eating them. And then, his wolf-appetite satisfied, he shifted back into human shape.

Shapeshifting itself was a complicated act, accompanied by carefully performed rituals. You could do it in many different ways. Gaius Petronius, a Roman who lived in the first century A.D., told a "transformation" story about a former slave named Niceros. Niceros, it seems, back in the days when he was still a slave, persuaded a young soldier to walk with him to his girl friend Melissa's house one moonlit night. After a while the soldier turned aside and when

Niceros looked to see where he had gone, he was understandably shaken to see that the soldier had stripped and was turning, little by little, into a wolf! When the soldier-wolf howled and ran off into the woods, Niceros took off, too, for Melissa's. When he arrived, he found her almost as upset as he was; a wolf, she told him, had just attacked her sheep, and even though a servant had wounded it in the neck, it had run off into the woods. Niceros, who by now was pretty sure he had put the whole thing together the right way, hurried off to check up on the soldier—and sure enough he found him home in bed, nursing a hurt neck!

The important thing about this transformation, and the thing it shares with most others, is that the werewolf had to strip before he could change. This is for an excellent reason, explained humorously in a modern story called "The Compleat Werewolf" by Anthony Boucher. When the hero, Professor Wolfe Wolf, who has become a werewolf for fun, forgets to take off his clothes before he shifts shape, he almost chokes on his collar as his neck thickens into a wolf's, and he gets horribly tangled up in his shirt and pants as he turns from a two-legged animal into a four-legged one!

It's important, in most werewolf stories, that the werewolf's clothes be nearby when he wants to change back into human shape. If they aren't, he has to stay a werewolf. There's a thirteenth-century French poem called "The Lay of Bisclaveret," written by Marie de France, which tells of a trick played on a werewolf by his beautiful but unloving wife. The lady's husband, says the poem, leaves her alone for three nights every week but when she asks him why, he refuses to explain. Finally she gets the truth out of him: on those nights, he becomes a wolf. The lady—who is secretly in love with another man, a handsome knight—isn't as unhappy to hear that as her husband might wish. She asks him if he has to undress to become a wolf, and if so where he puts his clothes. Naturally at first he doesn't want to answer, but after a while he tells her. She, of course, hides his clothes the first chance she gets and goes merrily off with her knight.

She doesn't get away with it for long, though. The king, out hunting one day, comes upon the werewolf-husband, who acts so much like a tame dog that the king is entranced and takes him home. The werewolf becomes his favorite pet, and is so gentle that he is loved by everyone at court. After some time the king gives a party and the werewolf's wife and her lover are among the guests. The werewolf takes one look at the conniving couple and turns from a gentle pet into a savage wild beast. A wise man figures out what has happened and forces the wife to confess. She and her lover are banished, but first she is made to tell where she hid her husband's clothes. They are found and brought to him, and his true shape is at last restored.

There are numerous other rituals connected with shapeshifting. In many parts of the world, it is believed that the werewolf must smear himself with a special ointment after he has taken off his clothes. The ingredients of the ointment vary, although most come from plants. Here are a few:

aconite (monkshood or wolfsbane)
belladonna
children's blood
children's fat
hemlock
poplar leaves
soot
cowbane
cinquefoil
oil
bats' blood
deadly nightshade

sweet flag
henbane
parsley
opium
mandrake

After rubbing his skin till it tingled with a heady ointment made from at least some of these ingredients, the werewolf put on a wolfskin or a belt made of wolf or human skin. There were exact directions for making these intricately designed belts. For example, if human skin was used, it usually had to be that of a murderer, and as wide as three fingers held together. In Germany, the belt had to be made from the skin of a hanged man; in Scandinavia, it often had magic signs engraved on it, plus a buckle with seven catches. (To change back to a person, all the werewolf had to do was break this buckle.) In other places, when a werewolf put on his special belt, he could not change into wolf-shape until he had put the buckle into the ninth hole.

After putting on his belt or skin, the werewolf had to chant a spell in order to make his transformation complete. The words of these spells are closely guarded but here is one:

In the ocean sea, on the island Buyán, in the
open plain, shines the moon upon an aspen stump,
into the green wood, into the spreading vale.
Around the stump goes a shaggy wolf; under his
teeth are all the horned cattle; but into the
wood the wolf goes not; into the vale the wolf
does not roam. Moon! moon! golden horns!
Melt the bullet, blunt the knife, rot the cudgel,
strike fear into man, beast, and reptile,
so that they may not seize the grey wolf, nor tear

37

from him his warm hide. My word is firm,
firmer than sleep or the strength of heroes.°

While reciting his spell, the werewolf had to stand in the middle of a magic circle. Sometimes all he had to do was draw any old circle around himself, strip, and presto-chango, he'd be a wolf. But other folk stories said that the circle had to be of a certain size, or that there should be two circles, one within the other. In that case, the magic shapeshifting ointment had to be cooked in a cauldron placed in the exact center of the circles, and the werewolf could not leave their boundaries until he had completed all parts of the ritual.

According to other beliefs, it was even easier to become a werewolf. All you had to do was eat roast wolf; or eat, or even just smell, certain powerful herbs; or drink water out of a wolf's footprint. Putting on a shirt made of wolfskin could automatically turn one into a wolf for a term of nine days. Where werebears, instead of werewolves, were popular, it was thought that a person could become a she-bear by putting a piece of wood into his mouth; to change back, all he had to do was spit out the wood. Rolling around in the dirt, naked and under a full moon, was also a favorite technique.

The full moon plays a big part in shapeshifting. In Sicily, anyone who slept outside in the full moon on Friday night became a wolf. In France as late as the early 1800's people believed that every time the moon was full certain people had to become wolves—especially priests' sons. To do this, they swam across a special pond, put on wolfskins which they found on the opposite shore, and roamed around all night long as wolves. By sunrise, to change back, they had to reverse the process.

In Arcadia, a part of ancient Greece well known for its were-

---

°From *The Werewolf* by Montague Summers (taken from *Songs of the Russian People* by W. R. Ralston). Published by arrangement with Lyle Stuart.

Cauchemar (*Nightmare*) by Laurence Housman. Shapeshifting, a complicated act, was accompanied by numerous rituals, often involving a wolf-skin.

wolves, members of a certain family (like the family cursed by St. Patrick in Ireland) were required to choose one of themselves to be a werewolf every so often. The method of change was similar to the French one: the chosen person would be escorted to a pond, he would strip and hang his clothes on an oak tree and swim across. Once on the other side, he would be a wolf. He was required to stay a wolf for nine years—longer if he killed and ate a human being. If he kept away from human flesh for the whole term, however, he could swim back across the pond, pick up his clothes (what was left of them after nine years) and, whammo! instant person.

To change back to human shape, a werewolf usually had to reverse whatever he'd done to become a wolf. Or he could roll in the dew, or go swimming, or wash, or—if he was patient—kneel in one place for one hundred years. Some werewolves didn't have to do anything at all; they changed back into humans automatically at sunrise.

Nonwerewolves could change werewolves back into human shape, too—a handy thing to know if you ran into one unexpectedly. As soon as most werewolves were wounded, for example, they turned back into human shape. Making the sign of the cross near a werewolf or calling him by his human name was supposed to work, if the name used was the one the werewolf was baptized with, and if it was repeated three times. You could also take three drops of blood from the werewolf (if he held still long enough without attacking), or hit his forehead three times with a knife.

One of the most risky methods of changing—for werewolves— was by means of a spell. It was easy enough for a werewolf to recite a spell while he was in human shape and thereby change into a wolf—but it was much harder for him to say the words in wolf-shape and change back. Most werewolves who used spells had to have someone else change them back—and that wasn't always possible. It wasn't in the case of one poor man in India who was a weretiger. The person who knew his spell died while the weretiger was in human shape. This left him with no way to change back when he again wished to be a tiger. He finally solved the problem—or so he thought—by teaching the spell to his wife. When he went up to her as a tiger, though, expecting her to say the spell and change him back, she didn't recognize him and began to scream. The more he tried to show her that he was human, the more she screamed. At last he grew so angry that he killed her. Too late he realized what he had done—spoiled his only chance of ever being in human shape again. For the rest of his life he remained a very bitter, people-hating tiger.

Most people nowadays believe that shapeshifting is impossible. But back in the old days, especially in the Middle Ages, shapeshifting was considered a very real and serious problem, especially by the Christian Church. Somehow the idea of changing from one shape to another seemed very like creation, and only God was supposed to be able to create. Since werewolves and other semihuman creatures were usually evil, churchmen reasoned that they couldn't be creations of God's. As evil beings they had to "belong" to the Devil—but the Devil, according to the beliefs of the times, couldn't create. Some Church authorities finally got around this awkward situation by saying that the Devil was *responsible* for shifting people into animal-shapes—but that he was only able to do this if God gave him permission! (Why God would do that in the first place isn't clear; the explanations given didn't go into that.)

God's permission or not, most werewolves who were captured, especially around the Middle Ages, were dealt with harshly. One of the most famous ones of all time, Peter Stumpe, was believed to be so much under the Devil's influence that he was cruelly tortured as well as executed:

Peter Stumpe lived near Cologne, Germany, in the late 1500's.

According to a pamphlet written a few months after his execution, Stumpe had practiced "wicked Artes"—the Devil's work—from the age of twelve on. He had an arrangement, so the pamphlet says, whereby he gave his soul and body to the Devil and the Devil gave him anything he wanted. What he wanted was to be able to change into animal-shape and attack people. The Devil gave him a belt which changed him into a wolf every time he put it on, and back to a man when he took it off.

Peter Stumpe started by murdering, in wolf-shape, anyone who displeased him, plus their relatives. Then, as he developed more and more of a taste for his wolflike habits, he fell upon just about anyone who caught his fancy, usually women or children. Often he went through the streets, well-dressed and polite, even saying hello to the friends and relatives of people he had murdered. Then, in wolf-shape, he would kill their lambs and goats, and their daughters, too, when he had the chance.

One day he met a woman and two men whom he wanted to kill. He couldn't take them all on at once, so he walked ahead where they couldn't see him and then called one of the men. When the man came, Stumpe attacked and killed him. The second man, just as Stumpe had hoped, set off to look for the first, and Stumpe killed him, too. By this time the woman suspected something was wrong. She tried to run away but Stumpe caught her, too—and both killed and ate her; at least people thought he did, since her body, unlike the bodies of the men, was never found.

By this time, things had gotten so bad that people's arms and legs were sometimes found lying around in fields after one of Stumpe's attacks. The terrified people still suspected a real wolf instead of a werewolf and it was a real wolf they hunted. One time a herd of cattle almost did the job of catching the culprit for them by stampeding in the middle of one of Stumpe's attacks. But he freed his

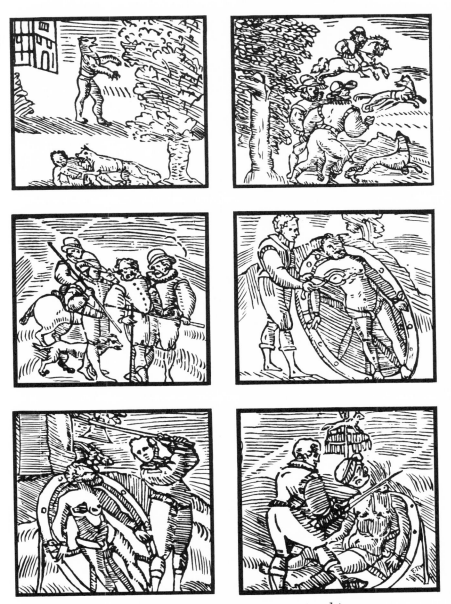

The Life and Death of Peter Stumpe, *printed in 1590.*

victim at the last minute and avoided being trampled to death just as the herd thundered toward him.

Day after day the people in the villages near Cologne tried to free themselves from the terrible creature that had them all trembling. They tried everything—hunting parties, dog packs, prayers—but the attacks went on. Peter Stumpe even managed to kill his own son (and, according to the pamphlet, devour his brains) without being suspected.

At last, though, his luck ran out, and the truth was revealed to the shocked villagers. A pack of excellent hunting dogs cornered Stumpe in the forest and, just as he slipped off his Devil's belt and turned back into human shape, the hunters came upon him. They hurried him off to the magistrate, now convinced that he, man and wolf, was the murderer they sought.

The magistrate, thinking Stumpe would deny the charges, ordered him tortured, but Stumpe, terrified, confessed both to being a werewolf and to having a pact with the Devil. He explained about his magic belt (which no one was ever able to find) and admitted that he had killed people and domestic animals while in wolf-shape. He—plus his daughter and a friend, who were supposed to have assisted him occasionally—were condemned to death. On October 28, 1589, after having his arms and legs broken and the flesh pulled off his bones, Peter Stumpe was beheaded and his body was burned. A monument was built in the town of Bedburg, where he was executed, consisting of a pole with a wooden wolf attached to it, plus the torture wheel on which Stumpe's body had been broken. As if that wasn't enough, Stumpe's head was displayed on a stake at the very top, and around the wheel were pieces of wood representing people he had killed. It certainly wouldn't be hard to think of more attractive monuments to set up in one's town square, but no doubt it served to remind people for some time to come that werewolfery, like crime, seldom paid!

III

CHARACTERISTICS OF WEREWOLVES

HERE'S OUR WEREWOLF NOW—not Peter Stumpe but any ordinary werewolf—having divested himself of his clothes, rubbed himself down with his ointment, and put on his wolfskin or wolfbelt. He has said the magic words and turned into a huge gray wolf. Now what?

Now he, free from the inhibitions and taboos of being a person, can do things no mere human ever could. Like Peter Stumpe, he may terrorize the countryside by murdering people and farm animals. But not all werewolves were cruel ravening beasts. A few liked wolf-shape simply because it allowed them to run freely through moonlit fields and forests, no longer burdened with human worries. Others used wolf-shape to enable them to do good deeds— like this semifictionalized account of a werewolf who knew William of Palermo.

One day long ago—probably in the early 1400's—young William, of royal blood, was playing outside in Palermo, on the island of Sicily. Unknown to him and to his parents there was an evil plot afoot. William's uncle, who wanted power over Sicily himself, had talked two women into murdering William—and even now, while William was playing, they crept stealthily up on him. Just in time a werewolf darted out of the forest and snatched the little boy in his teeth. He swiftly ran all the way across the island to Messina—a considerable distance—and jumped into the strait that separates Sicily from Italy. Then, still carrying the boy, he ran north to a woods near Rome where he at last put him down. Tenderly, the wolf took care of William, getting him food and keeping him warm and safe. In human form, this kindly werewolf was really a royal prince, Alfonso of Spain. Alfonso had a special reason for sympathizing with William. His wicked stepmother, who wanted her own son Braundinis to rule Spain, had changed Alfonso into a wolf to get rid of him!

One day while Alfonso-the-werewolf was off hunting food for William, a cowherd strayed into the forest and found the boy. He took him home and proceeded to bring him up as his own son. William didn't stay long in his new home, however. The emperor of Rome and his hunting party ran into him one day, and the emperor thought he was so handsome and pleasant and well-mannered that he took him to his palace and made him a page to his daughter Melior—who fell in love with him as soon as they were both old enough.

Well, the emperor thought it was one thing for William to be his daughter's page but quite another for him to be her husband—especially since she had already been promised to Braundinis, half brother to Alfonso-werewolf.

To keep Melior from being forced to marry Braundinis, William took her off into the forest. (They went, although the story doesn't explain why, disguised as white bears.) There Alfonso-werewolf, who had been keeping track of William with fatherly concern, set himself up as provider, robbing travelers in order to get rich and elegant food for the royal couple.

Before long, Melior's father got wind of where they were and sent out his troops—plus Braundinis—to chase them. Alfonso, ever faithful, led them back to Palermo where William, wearing a shield with a werewolf painted on it, fought Braundinis and won. Then he ordered Alfonso's wicked stepmother to dissolve the werewolf charm, which she did by tying a magic ring around his neck with a thread of red silk and reading charms aloud from an ancient book. Alfonso turned back into his rightful shape and William, to reward him for all his help, made him a knight. William and Melior got married and they all lived happily ever after—not to mention prosperously, for William eventually became emperor of Rome, and Alfonso took his rightful place as king of Spain.

Good werewolves like Alfonso, though, were far fewer in number than evil ones. Much more typical is the story, again from Italy, of the rich man who, whenever the moon was full, turned into a wolf. He confided his trouble to a servant who let him out of the house whenever he shifted his shape. Then, as a wolf, this respected nobleman roamed the city, terrorizing the inhabitants. At last one night a brave young man whom he was about to attack slashed him with his sword. As his blood (which the story says was thick and unnaturally dark) poured out, the werewolf howled in pain—and the nobleman's face and body broke through the wolf disguise. Luckily he recovered from his wounds and never again suffered from werewolfery, much to the relief of both himself and his neighbors.

Wounding a werewolf, besides freeing it from its spell, is also a foolproof method of exposing its human identity. In almost all parts of the world a were-animal, wounded in animal-shape, will keep the same wound in the same part of its body when it is in human shape. (Malaysian werewolves are an exception. Some of them can't be wounded at all while in wolf-shape.) This can have embarrassing consequences. A prince in India, for example, once found a fox asleep in his chrysanthemum bed. He took a shot at it, wounding it

In the seventeenth century it was believed that witches used animals for a variety of purposes. This one seems to have included a werewolf among her "familiars."

in the forehead—and later, much to his horror, discovered that his girl friend had a gunshot wound in her forehead. Similarly, in Guiana, a young man out hunting was surprised to see a tiger, which he had hit in the jaw with a bone-tipped arrow, raise its paw in an untigerlike way and break the arrow off before he trotted away into the jungle. The next day the young man's father complained of a sore mouth. Imagine his horror when he found a piece of bone from his arrow tip embedded deeply in his father's mouth!

Saddest of all, though, is a story which comes from sixteenth-century France. A certain gentleman asked a hunter he knew to bring him something choice from his day's bag. The hunter agreed and set off. Before the day had really begun, he was attacked by a huge wolf. He quickly fired at the beast but—perhaps because he was so frightened or so taken by surprise—he missed. The wolf, undaunted by the sound of gunfire, leaped at the hunter and the hunter, throwing his gun aside, groped quickly for his knife. Just in time he got it out and slashed at the wolf. The wolf yelped in pain and limped away—leaving one of its paws in the hunter's hand!

Feeling he'd had enough adventures for one day, the hunter put the wolf's paw into his game bag and went back to tell the gentleman about his bad luck.

"And look what I have here," he said to the gentleman when he'd reached the end of his story. "The very paw of the wolf that attacked me." With a flourish, he opened his bag and pulled out—not the wolf's paw but the slender, beringed hand of a woman.

The hunter stared at the hand in disbelief but his disbelief was nothing compared to the gentleman's shock. "Let me see that," he said in a hoarse whisper. After peering closely at a ring on one of the perfectly shaped fingers, he went hurrying out of the room to find his wife.

He found her, all right—with a shawl wrapped around the end of one of her arms. "And what has happened to your hand?" the gentleman asked her, trying to keep his voice steady. "Oh, nothing," she said, holding her arm behind her back—but he reached for her grimly and removed the shawl. There, sure enough, was the mutilated stump of her wrist.

Not long after that, the wife confessed that she was a werewolf and that she had attacked the hunter. Her fate: to be burned at the stake for witchcraft.

Les Lupins (The Wolves) by Maurice Sand. According to Lithuanian legend, at Christmastime witches in wolf-shape would meet at an old castle, where they had to prove their strength by jumping over a wall.

Some werewolves, especially in the Middle Ages, were actually more witch than wolf. Witches were supposed to be able to change their shapes at will and, although most preferred to become cats, some occasionally chose to be wolves. According to Lithuanian legend, every year at Christmastime a young lame boy would go from house to house gathering together all the Devil-worshipers. These witches—for, of course, witches were worshipers of the Devil—came out of their houses and, in wolf-shape, spent the next twelve days preying on sheep and cattle—doing, some say, far more damage than real wolves. Only rarely did one of them refuse to go on this rampage, for those who hung back were severely beaten by their leader, a man who carried a brutal whip with pieces of iron tied onto it.

In another version of the same legend, the witch-werewolves were said to eat people as well as sheep and cattle. They drank a lot of beer, too, and gathered at a certain ruined castle, where they had to prove their strength by jumping over a wall. Any weakling who didn't make it was beaten and killed.

In Normandy, northern France, it was believed that werewolves (*loups garous*, the French called them) were given a special skin by the Devil, and were beaten by the Devil every time they came upon a roadside cross. In Poland it was believed that a witch could change an entire wedding party into wolves if she put a belt made of human skin over the threshold of the house in which the wedding was taking place. Anyone who stepped over it was turned into a wolf—and, what's more, he stayed that way for three years. If, at the end of three years, the witch remembered to put a skin over the werewolf with the hair facing out, he could be human again. Once, though, the witch involved picked a skin that was too small—and an unhappy bridegroom emerged, his wolf's tail still hanging out behind. He had to go through the rest of his life with a tail attached to his otherwise human back end!

Witch-werewolves usually ended up an evening's feasting by gathering together at the sabbat. According to some stories, they brought with them the insides of their victims as offerings to their Devil god.

There has always been a connection between witches and water. In England and Germany, for example, a sure test for finding out if someone was a witch was to throw her into a lake or pond. Water, it was believed, wouldn't support witches—so if a woman sank in the water, she was considered a witch. (One wonders how many women knew how to swim in those days!) Although many werewolves had to swim in order to shapeshift, others, especially witch-werewolves, feared it. The Christmas werewolves in Lithuania had so much trouble crossing water that their leader had to part streams for them (by hitting the water with his whip) so they could walk across without getting wet.

Witch-werewolves were likely to enjoy their werewolfery and to have chosen it freely. But most ordinary werewolves were changed against their wills. They became wolves by accident or because the Devil or someone else had forced them into it. These, unlike witch-werewolves, were often very religious—like this werewolf couple:

In Ireland, many centuries ago, a priest was traveling in a thick wood. He had just built himself a friendly fire and had begun to settle down for the night when he was terrified to see a huge gray wolf coming toward him out of the underbrush. As he was sitting there wondering if it would be safer to sit still, climb a tree, or run, the wolf amazed him by speaking: "Don't be afraid," he said. "I won't hurt you. But please, please, help me!"

It took the priest a few minutes to get hold of himself, but finally he was able to say, "What's the matter? And who are you? How can you talk like a man and look like a wolf?"

Sadly, but not without some haste, the wolf explained that his family was living under a curse (perhaps St. Patrick's, but the story doesn't say that) which required two of them to become wolves every seven years. Any couple who lived through a seven-year period as wolves could then return to human shape, and be replaced by another couple.

"My wife," the wolf went on, "who shares my unhappy fate, is very ill. I beg you to come with me and give her the last rites so that if she dies in this terrible shape she may at least have a chance of being received into heaven."

The priest had his doubts about the wolf's story but didn't dare refuse. He followed the creature a little farther into the forest and sure enough, they soon came to a tree under which lay a female wolf, groaning and sighing like a sickly human woman.

The priest heard the she-wolf's confession and did what he could for her, but he did not dare give her the sacred sacrament of Communion, in case she was really a creature of the Devil. "I cannot," he said. "I haven't the right things with me." The male wolf, however, pointed to a container around the priest's neck which indeed held some holy wafers—so the priest could no longer say that he didn't have the equipment necessary to carry out the ceremony. Then the male wolf, to prove that he and his wife were really what they claimed to be, folded down some of his wife's pelt, so that the priest could see she was really a human being underneath. At last convinced—though still shaken—the priest gave the she-wolf Communion. The male wolf then thanked him gratefully and led him safely out of the forest. Unfortunately one can only guess as to the fate of the sick she-wolf; the story doesn't go any further.

Unwilling werewolves did not always know that they would be wolves only for certain periods of time. Others, like the soldier Raimbaud de Poinet of France, had to depend on chance to free them from their despised shapes. Raimbaud was banished by a cer-

A witch returning from the sabbat in the shape of a wolf.

tain nobleman and one night while he was wandering lonely in his exile, he suddenly felt odd and was horrified to observe that he was slowly changing into a wolf. Once the change was complete, he couldn't help but return to his own village, the place he knew best. There, he fell upon small children and helpless old people with true wolflike fury. Finally a carpenter attacked him, cutting off a hind paw—and Raimbaud immediately turned back into a man. He was so happy to be himself again that he said he didn't mind at all having lost one foot.

Another poor man had suffered from werewolfery since childhood. Unlike Raimbaud, he knew what to expect, but the fact that

54

he turned into a wolf regularly at a certain hour of the night complicated his life somewhat. He had always managed to hide his werewolfery from everyone, even his own wife, whom he loved dearly. But one night he and his wife went to a party. They had such a good time that the werewolf forgot to keep an eye on the clock and, though he hurried his wife away abruptly hoping to get them both home before the transformation took place, it soon became obvious that he just plain wasn't going to make it. "Here," he said, handing his wife the reins of their horse-drawn cart, "wait for me." He told her that if any creature came up to her she should hit it with her apron. Then he hurried into the woods.

The poor wife was confused by these directions, not to mention her husband's behavior, but nevertheless she sat there patiently waiting for her husband to return. Within a few minutes, a savage gray wolf came leaping at her out of the forest. Remembering what her husband had told her, she summoned up her courage and hit at the beast with her apron—though she couldn't help thinking it seemed a very flimsy weapon. Much to her surprise, however, the wolf immediately calmed down. He seized a piece of her apron in his mouth and ran back into the forest—but the wife was so grateful and so amazed at having been spared that instead of wondering about the wolf's strange retreat, all she could do was be thankful to her husband for giving her the directions that had obviously saved her life.

Not long after that the woman's husband came back, grinning in an embarrassed way and holding a piece of his wife's torn apron in his mouth. Instantly, the wife understood—and stifled a scream, for how would she ever know, from this day on, when her husband might turn into a wolf and attack her again?

"No, no, my dear," he reassured her, climbing back into his seat and taking the reins as if nothing had happened. "It's all right now. In fact, you have freed me from this horrible curse."

Indeed, she had, for, perhaps because of his wife's trust and loyalty, this man never again became a wolf.

Many folk legends say that werewolves turn into wolves only at certain times—like when the moon is full. Peasants in Denmark believed that some people turned into three-legged dogs at a particular time of night. In Poland, werewolves turned to wolves only in the middle of the summer and at Christmas. A Moslem doctor, Avicenna, who lived in the eleventh century A.D., said that werewolfery was most common in the month of February—a belief shared by many people in many parts of the world. In rural Italy it was believed that anyone born on Christmas night would become a wolf at that time every year. In some places, because of this, little wax crosses were put up near roadside shrines especially at Christmas— a werewolf, the peasants believed, wouldn't be able to do anything evil near one of those crosses.

In Sicily, there were dozens of wolf and werewolf superstitions, some of which were similar to those in other countries. Anyone seen by a werewolf, said the Sicilians, would lose his power of speech (no wonder, if werewolves are as scary as they are said to be). Anyone who had a lot of aches and pains should carry a wolf's foot; it would make him feel better. Anyone who wanted to be especially brave and strong should wear a wolf's skin. *But*—anyone who ate wolf meat would always be hungry.

As the moon got larger each month, Sicilian werewolves grew restless. Slowly, slowly they changed—first groveling in the mud with sunken, glazed eyes, then quivering, and finally leaping up with an earsplitting howl. Luckily Sicilian werewolves howled so much that they warned everyone they were around. They were also afraid of light—so they were fairly easy to control. Sometimes, too, a Sicilian werewolf even warned his friends and family that he was due to change so that they could protect themselves. He would warn them especially not to open their doors if he called to them, unless he called three times; after that, it would be safe for them to let him in, for he would have lost his power and would no longer be able to harm them.

A Sicilian werewolf could be freed from his spell if you hit him with a knife on the head—but hitting him with a stick did no good at all; it had to be a knife. Sometimes he could also be freed if someone cut the backs of his front paws.

In Messina, on the side of Sicily nearest the mainland, a werewolf could be brought out of his spell if he was hit with a specially shaped key. But elsewhere on the island, there was nothing that could be done against werewolves at all.

In Ireland or Scotland, you could sometimes hold a werewolf off by protecting yourself with a branch of a yew tree, a piece of mistletoe, or an ash twig. You could also get yourself on the other side of a running stream for it was unlikely that these werewolves could cross water.

To free a Danish werewolf from his spell, all you had to do was say something like, "Hey I know you're a werewolf, and I think that's terrible." As if his wolfish feelings were hurt, the werewolf would then quietly change back into a person.

It is mostly in the movies that you need special equipment for killing or wounding a werewolf. Most of the time, all you had to do was go after it as you would any other animal. But in some places, Scotland, for instance, just like in the movies, you needed a silver bullet, a bullet blessed by a clergyman, or a silver dagger.

In Ireland, "The Wolf Land," some poor souls were said to become wolves whenever they bit anything—which must have made them unpopular as dinner guests. Many Irish werewolves, like those in the story of the priest and the werewolf couple, were victims of hereditary curses. An old poem, dating from the thirteenth century, spoke of the special shapeshifting ability certain men had "which comes to them from their forebears." According to the poem, these Irish werewolves had to stay wolves forever if they were touched even lightly by their friends. They used to warn their friends whenever they were going to shift shape, and they tried to do it fairly far away from home in order to reduce the chance of being locked into wolf-shape forever by a friendly—or a not-so-friendly—pat.

In Serbia werewolves must have been pretty easy to get rid of— for they held yearly meetings, so the story goes, and hung their skins up on nearby trees. If the villagers could only find out where they met, all they had to do was sneak up, take the skins away, and burn

A werewolf from a thirteenth-century bestiary manuscript.

them, and all the werewolves would be forced to return to human shape. (According to some werewolf superstitions, burning or otherwise destroying the wolfskin would kill the werewolf.)

The werewolf is not always 100 percent like a real wolf, although you'd have to look pretty closely to see the difference. In some stories, for instance, the werewolf is bigger than any ordinary wolf would be. In others, its eyes remain human, and in still others, it has no tail. Frequently, if something happens to alter the transformation either to or from wolf-shape, or if the wolf is hurt, the human form will break through the wolf form, resulting in a grotesque-looking creature that is part wolf, part human being. To tell if a wolf is a real wolf or a werewolf, it is recommended that you throw a piece of iron or steel at the suspected creature. If it is a werewolf, its wolfskin will instantly open at the forehead, and the person will emerge.

Clauda Gaillard, a famous French werewolf, was said to have had no tail. A neighbor of hers, Jeanne Perrin, saw her in wolf-shape one day, and realized she was not a real wolf because her hind legs hadn't changed—only the rest of her.

In Portugal, werewolves were called *lobis-homems*. One kind of lobis-homem, most common in the 1400's, was really quite a gentle beast, even a little sad. Under a spell, this lobis-homem unhappily went off at night to a place where four roads met. There it turned around five times, faster, faster, faster, until it finally fell down on the ground. By this time, the poor creature was howling—perhaps with dizziness, perhaps with frustration at being driven to act in such an unhuman way. Then, after groveling around in the dirt for a while, the lobis-homem stood up and changed into a wolf—or into whatever wild animal had lain upon the spot (it must have been especially frightening not to know what you were going to turn into). The beast then ran through the countryside, howling pitifully and hurting no one. This kind of lobis-homem seems to have been a timid beast as well as a sad one; light terrified him, and he loped off into the woods at the first faint flicker. Peasants who heard him whining, making a throaty, sobbing noise, told each other, "The lobis-homem wants us to blow out the candle." If a peasant met this kind of lobis-homem on a dark, lonely road, he was rarely afraid, for he knew all he had to do was strike a light or hold up his lantern and the animal would run away.

How did you recognize this lobis-homem if you were that peasant on the lonely road? By his short tail, covered with yellow fur.

Not all Portuguese lobis-homems were gentle and sad, however. There was an evil variety, too, although this kind was less common. The evil lobis-homem was definitely connected with witchcraft, as this story shows:

In the wilds of Portugal, a young farmer's wife was about to have her first child. The young husband sent his servant out to hire a girl to help with his wife's chores while she was indisposed. "Take the first likely-looking girl you see," he told the servant, who did just that.

The girl he hired was named Joanna; the servant had found her sitting alone by the side of the road, wearing a brown cloak which she held closely around her. Oddly enough, she said she was looking for a job as a servant girl and wanted to work in that very area. She was, he thought, a very "likely-looking girl"—what he could see of her under the cloak—and she had, he noticed once when the cloak slipped, unusual-looking eyes.

When he brought her home, however, the neighbors did not seem to share his enthusiasm. They said she seemed strange to them, though they couldn't explain why. But the young farmer hired Joanna without question, so the servant felt he had done his job well enough.

Joanna turned out to be a great help around the house. Soon the farmer's wife had her baby—a healthy, strong little boy. To be sure, an old wise woman who lived nearby took one look at the infant and said, "He is bewitched!" but no one paid any attention; she was always saying strange things and muttering darkly to herself. "He has the Devil's mark," the old woman insisted, shaking a wizened finger. At that, someone examined the baby and did find a little half-moon-shaped freckle between his shoulders—but that, they thought, did not have to mean a thing. The baby's parents, though, could not dismiss it so easily, and asked the old wise woman what they should do. "It will be all right," she told them, soothed at being consulted, "as long as you keep your eye on him every time there is a full moon."

The young parents watched their child carefully at each full moon and for a time all was well. Joanna went about her business quietly—except when the old wise woman came to call. Then Joanna found some excuse to go out or sat hunched in a corner, her brown cloak pulled up around her face. She minded the farmer and his wife, however, and the farmer's wife grew so fond of her that she confided in her. What did it matter if Joanna didn't like the old wise woman, who was a queer duck anyway, or if she lost her temper now and then and allowed her strangely shaped eyes to blaze in hot fury? Other people had tempers; one should take people as they were, not as one wished them to be.

At length, the farmer's wife told Joanna what the wise woman had said about the mark on the little boy, expecting the girl to laugh at it or be afraid. She did neither, much to her mistress's surprise. She even said that she knew what it was.

"What?" asked the anxious mother, for the wise woman had not told her.

"It is the mark," said Joanna calmly, "of the lobis-homem. The boy will be one by the time he is sixteen."

At this the young mother became frantic, as one might well expect. She asked Joanna if there was anything she and her husband could do to prevent this tragedy from befalling their innocent son. "Yes," said Joanna—and explained.

The mother was to kill a white pigeon, and cover the half-moon mark with its blood so the mark could no longer be seen. Then she was to put the baby, naked, on a soft blanket and lay him on the mountain when the moon next rose before midnight. "The moon," Joanna explained, "will suck up the mark the way it sucks up the sea when the tide turns."

Of course the young parents, anxious to save their boy from the curse of being a werewolf, did exactly what their servant girl told them to do. As he lay his son on the blanket where the new moon's pale light would fall on him, the young farmer said, "I hope there are not any wolves around tonight."

"Come, come," said the friends who had gone with him to the mountain. "You know perfectly well there hasn't been a wolf seen here in years."

Still, the young farmer loaded his gun, just in case, as soon as he got home.

And no sooner had he done so than he saw, just as the moon rose, a huge wolf standing over his child. Yelling, he ran toward the beast and fired—but the animal had already done its worst; its jaws were dripping with blood and the baby, alas, lay dead. As the wolf slunk away, someone managed to club it on its right front leg—but that didn't stop it from skulking away into the underbrush.

For a while the family was too distraught over the death of the baby to notice, but finally someone remarked that Joanna seemed to be nowhere about. How odd this was, since it had been she who had suggested that the child be taken to the mountain in the first place, and since she had always seemed so fond of him!

Then suddenly the farmer and his wife realized the awful truth and saw how they had been deceived. At dawn the farmer and some

Although wolf attacks on people were rare, they made dramatic subjects for artists and storytellers.

neighbors went back out to the mountain and sure enough, near where the child had been murdered was Joanna, lying wounded on the bloody ground, with a badly bruised right arm. "I had hidden here to make sure he would be all right," she protested, "and ran out to save him when the wolf came. I was hit when you fired at the wolf—that's why there is so much blood on me." But when they asked her to show them a gunshot wound, and when they asked her how she had bruised her arm, recalling that the wolf had been beaten with a club, she had nothing to say.

The good people sent for a priest for Joanna, but she died before he came. The wise woman showed them, before they buried her on the mountainside, that Joanna also had the same half-moon mark on her body. "She was a witch," the wise woman said, "a lobis-homem herself," and she told them that had Joanna ever let her look at her eyes she would have known for sure, for all lobis-homems had eyes shaped exactly like hers.

The sad thing was that the wise woman also told them that if a lobis-homem can drink the blood of a baby it has just killed, it can be freed from its evil spell. So Joanna was another reluctant werewolf, driven to evil by a spell she had not chosen to be under.

In Portugal, as the wise woman said, you could recognize a lobis-homem because of the shape of his or her eyes. In many other countries, a wise woman would have looked at eyebrows instead, for the brows of many werewolves, in human shape, were unusually thick and bushy and grew straight across, meeting over the bridge of the nose.

Curved fingernails, long and reddish in color, were another sure sign of werewolfery in some areas, as were low-set ears or unusual hairiness. Werewolves were also said to have hairs growing out of the palms of their hands and to have scratches all over their legs and arms, because in wolf-shape they had run through thick brambly underbrush.

A long index finger, or a long third finger, was another sign. So was a Devil's mark. Sometimes this was a half-moon shape like the one in the Portuguese story, and sometimes it was a pentagram (five-pointed star). In some movies—but few legends—if a werewolf saw a pentagram in the palm of a person's hand he knew that person would be his next victim.

An extra-thin face, sunken eyes, poor eyesight, dryness of the mouth or extreme thirst, broad hands, paleness—all these were considered signs, too. But the most interesting is that in countries where most people are dark-haired and dark-skinned, light-haired and light-skinned people were considered likely to be werewolves (or vampires and other evil creatures). In places where most people are light-haired and light-skinned, dark people were suspect. Suspicion also fell on people who were mentally or physically handicapped in some way—on anyone, in short, who was "different."

Unfortunately, "different" people have always been singled out for ridicule or suspicion. Perhaps this was the reason that the people of Arcadia, in ancient Greece, got a reputation for being a race of werewolves—because they were "different."

IV
ORIGINS

TODAY, the name "Arcadia" (or "Arcady") immediately calls up images of green, daisy-decked pastures, flocks of gentle sheep, and beribboned shepherdesses pining over handsome pipe-playing shepherd lads. But back in the old days, when the Greeks believed in a hierarchy of demanding gods, Arcadia was far from a lovely pastoral idyll. It was, in fact, a place where wolves ravaged flocks of peacefully grazing sheep, and where gory human sacrifices were made to the gods. The Arcadians themselves were said to be the bloodthirstiest of cannibals.

The basic Arcadian werewolf story is about Zeus, head of all the gods, and Lycaon, king of Arcadia, a cruel tyrant who permitted all kinds of evil to flourish under his reign. According to Ovid, a famous Roman poet who lived around the time of Christ's birth, Zeus heard rumors of the wickedness rampant in Arcadia. Disguised as a mortal man, he went down to earth to investigate. Everything he saw proved the rumors were true; in fact, Zeus was shocked and angered to find that the situation was even worse than he had heard.

At last he was ready to face King Lycaon and accuse him of being the evil tyrant that he was. He went to his palace and, as he prepared to enter, let it be known that he was a god. Arcadian subjects standing nearby fell to their knees respectfully and began to pray. But the wicked Lycaon only laughed. "Perhaps he is a god and perhaps not," he said disrespectfully. "I shall test him and find out."

Lycaon hurried off to prepare his test: he would try to murder Zeus in his sleep. A god, of course, would be able to survive such a test; a mortal man would not.

Zeus, since he was a god, realized what was going on, but decided to say nothing. At dinner, though, he could no longer keep his temper. Lycaon, bloodthirsty brute that he was, murdered a peaceful messenger sent from another kingdom—murdered him, boiled him, and served him to Zeus for dinner. At this, Zeus flew into a rage and turned Lycaon into a wolf—except for his eyes, which, like those of many other werewolves, stayed human.

From then on, Arcadia had a reputation for werewolfery as well as for cruelty. A cult developed out of the Lycaon story, and a festival to Zeus was held there every nine years. It was a grisly occasion during which a certain family had to choose one of their members to be a wolf until the next festival. This person had to swim across a lake and stay a wolf—without eating human flesh—until his nine-year term was up. (This may or may not have been the origin of the similar Irish story—but it certainly is a lot like it.)

Arcadia's notoriety grew and grew. Soon it was said that the people there not only made human sacrifices, but that they ate human flesh as well. Not only did one of their number turn into a wolf periodically, but they all worshiped wolves instead of gods. Rumor had it that a certain Arcadian once tasted the flesh of a boy who had been sacrificed; he instantly turned into a wolf. Some sources explain these rumors of werewolfery by saying that the priests who conducted sacrifices in Arcadia dressed in wolfskins while performing their rites. A horrified outsider, not understanding that, could easily have imagined that the priests indeed had become wolves,

Le Meneu' de Loups (*The Wolf Leader*) *by Maurice Sand.*

just as ancient tribesmen in other parts of the world may occasionally have believed that their priests and ceremonial dancers and hunters were the animals they represented.

Wicked King Lycaon and later wolf-worshiping Arcadians were by no means the only shapeshifters in the days of the Greek and Roman gods. Gods often disguised themselves as animals so they could walk among mortals unobserved. Some say that the mother of Apollo, god of music, poetry, and the sun (among other things), was in the shape of a wolf when she gave birth to him, and that Apollo himself sometimes changed into a wolf.

As time went on, werewolf stories spread to pretty much all parts of the world where there were wolves—and where there weren't wolves, there were stories of other were-animals. Whether such stories spread by word of mouth or whether they grew up independently of each other is hard to say. Probably a bit of both. Fear is basic to all people, and fear of wild wolves is basic to most. People have always made up stories to explain things which are hard to understand. The mangled body of a peasant child lying in the mud with human footprints all around could lead a hysterical parent to say "He was killed by a man who was like a wolf." The winter wind howling through a lonely forest could make a woodcutter speculate on the possibility of there being extra-powerful wolves—wolves like gods or wolves like men. A hunted wolf who cleverly eludes his pursuers or lures them into a trap could easily be said to have the mind of a man. Experiences like these could have caused people in various parts of the world to develop their own werewolf legends independently of each other. Some stories must have developed this way; after all, people believed in werewolves long before the days of television, cars, planes, mail deliveries, telephones, and other means of communication.

However, the fact that werewolves in stories from various parts of the world have characteristics in common—like keeping the same wound in both human shape and wolf-shape—makes it sound as if word of mouth had a lot to do with it.

Traders were probably responsible for spreading some werewolf stories and for swapping werewolf superstitions with people in various countries. Most of the stories they told were bloody and horrifying, but once in a while there was one worthy of a chuckle. For instance, there's this one from the Byzantine Empire, between the Mediterranean and the Black Sea. The time: fourteenth century or earlier.

A clever thief once decided to stop at a certain inn to see what he could steal. Right away he spotted the innkeeper's fine cloak as a likely object. The only trouble was, the innkeeper never took his cloak off. Finally, after pondering the problem for a long time, the thief hit upon an ingenious plan. The very next day he went up to the innkeeper and pretended to engage him in friendly conversation. After they had talked of this and that, sitting side by side on one bench like two old cronies, the thief began to yawn. With the first yawn, he let out a long-drawn wolfish howl. "What on earth's the matter?" asked the innkeeper. "Are you tired?"

"No, no," said the thief, "nothing like that. But would you mind looking after my clothes for me? If I guess aright, I'm about to go wolfish—though why I should be so afflicted I will never know."

"Wolfish?" asked the innkeeper anxiously, as he tried to edge inconspicuously away from the thief.

"Yes," said the thief with another huge yawn. "It's happened a few times before. First I start feeling strange, and then I yawn, and then I yawn again, and then a third time and after the third—abracadabra—I turn into a wolf. You know, the kind that can't put up with ordinary fare like cattle and sheep, but who has to eat nice plump people, bones and all. Curious, isn't it? I'm really a very quiet sort of chap most of the time."

The innkeeper could stand no more and he jumped up to leave, his magnificent cloak billowing around him. But the thief grabbed hold of the cloak and said, "Oh, please, wait a minute, kind innkeeper. Let me give you my clothes to guard for me." He started undoing his garments, at the same time opening his mouth to begin the third yawn. The innkeeper needed no further warning. He pulled free—clean out of his precious cloak—and ran away, leaving the thief both happier and richer.

Although most of the werewolf stories we still know about today are of European or near-European origin, the belief was by no means limited to that part of the world. China and other Asian countries had their share of werewolf and other shapeshifting stories, some of them very similar to the European ones. There's this story of a Chinese woodcutter, for example:

A woodcutter was attacked one night by an enormous wolf and, in self-defense, he swung his axe at the beast, managing to cut him in the head. The wolf fell unconscious to the ground, stayed there until sunrise, and then disappeared. The woodcutter followed the wolf's trail the next morning—to the hut of a certain peasant, who was in bed nursing an axe wound in his forehead. The peasant's sons then killed their werewolf father who, dying, turned back into a wolf!

A forerunner of many later werewolf stories comes from the Norwegian and Icelandic saga of the Volsungs. Sigmund, son of King Volsung, who had seen his brothers eaten by a werewolf, was walking in the forest one day with his son Sinfjötli. They came upon a cottage, went inside, and found two men there, apparently asleep. Hanging on the wall above them were two wolfskins, for unknown to Sigmund and Sinfjötli, the sleeping men were really shapeshifters who were allowed to be human only every tenth day. This was the

Werewolf and other were-animal legends have arisen wherever fearsome

beasts have roamed. The dots indicate places where such stories exist.

tenth day, so they looked like men and had been able to cast aside their wolfish skins.

Sigmund and Sinfjötli knew only that these were good heavy pelts, such as might be useful in their harsh northern climate. Glad to have found such treasures, they put them on—and of course changed immediately into wolves themselves. Unlike some other werewolves, though, they could both speak like men and howl like wolves.

At first they tried to take the wolfskins off and become men again, but when they discovered they could not, they decided they might as well see what it was like to be wolves. They trotted deeper into the forest, each agreeing to howl for the other's assistance if he encountered more than seven men at a time.

Sigmund, the father, was the first to find a large group of men. He howled, Sinfjötli ran to his side, and together they killed the entire party with no trouble at all. Then they parted again, and soon Sinfjötli found a group of eleven men. He was young and strong and perhaps a bit of a show-off, so he killed them all without howling for his father.

After a while, Sigmund found Sinfjötli resting under a tree.

"Why didn't you howl?" he asked angrily. "You know our agreement!"

"Oh," said Sinfjötli breezily, "it was only eleven men; I needed no help for that!"

This made Sigmund angry and, wolflike, he bit Sinfjötli, giving him a grievous wound. Then he realized what he had done and, manlike, was sorry; Sinfjötli was, after all, his son. He picked Sinfjötli up and carried him home on his back, cursing the evil wolf-shapes for making him act so inhuman. And when he finally regained human shape, at the end of ten days, he burned both the skins so he and his son would never be tempted to become wolves again.

There's a much later Norwegian werewolf story on the old "love conquers all" theme, showing that the werewolf superstition lasted in Norway well into Christian times:

Lasse and his wife lived in a tiny village in the middle of a forest. Every day of his life Lasse had remembered to cross himself and say his prayers, but on this day for some reason he forgot. He thus became open to spells—and sure enough a witch found him and gleefully turned him into a wolf.

Year after year went by, and Lasse's good wife stayed home mourning him (for she believed he was dead) and keeping his memory alive. One Christmas Eve, a beggar woman came to the door, asking for food. The goodwife took her in, gave her a hearty meal, and was as kind to her as if she had been her sister. As she was leaving, the beggar woman, much to the wife's surprise, turned and said, "Your husband, you know, is not dead as you thought, but roams the forest as a wolf. You will probably see him again." Then, without giving the goodwife a chance to ask any questions, the beggar woman was gone.

That evening, the goodwife took a piece of meat for the next day's meal into her pantry. Just as she was leaving, she heard a noise and there was a wolf standing on the pantry steps, looking at her with lonely, hungry eyes. "You poor thing," said the wife, wondering why she did not feel terribly afraid. "If only I could be sure you were my husband and that the beggar was telling the truth, I would give you some meat."

Off fell the wolfskin—and Lasse and his wife had the happiest Christmas of their lives!

The Vikings of Scandinavia, historians believe, probably crossed over to North America long before Columbus arrived, and it is certainly possible that they communicated their werewolf superstitions to the many Indian tribes which were all over the continent. It seems more likely, however, that North American werewolf stories developed independently, with their roots in hunting rituals, ancestor worship, and the closeness early man felt to his animal neighbors.

Some of the most detailed North American werewolf stories have come from the Navajo Indians of the southwestern United States. Navajo werewolves, in addition to preying on sheep as real wolves did and killing and eating humans as werewolves did, also robbed graves, stealing the jewels that were buried with dead people. These werewolves, it was believed, caused sickness, especially tuberculosis. They would look down the roof holes of people's hogans—sometimes knocking four times, sometimes making a noise or prying some mud loose—but always the Navajo werewolf revealed himself to his victims with agonizing slowness. His burning eyes, perhaps, would be the first thing to appear in the roof hole, and then his head, and then, bit by bit, the rest of him. . . .

Navajo werewolves were said to have powers definitely connected with witchcraft. It was said that to kill their victims they sometimes made a strong powder from a man's finger and a girl's tongue mixed together. Then they would throw this deadly stuff over their victim, killing him.

How could a person tell if a fellow tribesman was a werewolf? One sure way was to look in his hogan for a wolfskin. If there was one there (or a mountain-lion skin), one could be sure that its owner was a were-creature.

Canada had werewolves, too. They seem related to both Navajo ones and French ones, which makes sense, since Canada is close enough to the United States to have been influenced by Indian lore from there. And Canada, since it was settled partly by French people, absorbed a good deal of French culture. A certain kind of Canadian werewolf, like the Navajo variety, was said to dig up graves. All

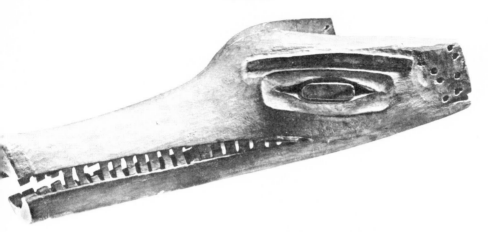

This Canadian Indian wolf mask, found in 1778, may be the oldest in existence.

Canadian werewolves were called the same thing they were in France: loups garous.

France. One could almost call that country the werewolf capital of the world—at least one could have during the late sixteenth and early seventeenth centuries. It was as if all the werewolf superstitions and fears the world had known for centuries came together in that one European country, and caused a kind of long-term hysteria.

V

AN EPIDEMIC OF WEREWOLVES

THE SIXTEENTH CENTURY was a bad time to be alive if one was terrified of werewolves or witches. Records of the time show that there were about thirty thousand cases of werewolfery between the years 1520 and 1630. Many of these were in France.

France in the sixteenth century was a place of great religious turmoil. Civil and religious wars, most between Catholics and Protestants, raged in the country. The officers of the Inquisition, a Catholic body which investigated reports of heresy and brought to trial those who did not believe in the Church's teachings, turned their power and their wrath against Protestants during the religious wars. Religious fervor was at such a height in this period that even animals were occasionally tried for sorcery. A rooster was burned at the stake in 1474 for having laid an egg. More mercy was shown to pigs, apparently; in 1457 a sow and six piglets were tried for having killed a child. Only the sow was executed—the judge felt that her piglets were too young to have known what they were doing!

Cases like this, though there weren't very many of them, continued into the sixteenth century. It is not surprising then that anyone suspected of the Satanic practice of shapeshifting was harshly treated, too.

You've already heard about Perrenette Gandillon, who was accused of killing Benedict Bidel, and her notorious relatives. And about Clauda Gaillard whose transformation into wolf-shape left her tailless. Clauda, like the Gandillons, was tried by Henri Bouget, the judge who passed sentence—severely—on many supposed witches and werewolves in sixteenth-century France. It is partly due to his careful record-keeping that so many werewolf stories have survived to this day.

But even before Benedict's case, there were other sensational werewolf trials. One of the first recorded ones was that of Pierre Burgot and Michel Verdun, who were tried in 1521.

The courtroom was packed for several days while people listened spellbound to "Gross Pierre's" gory tale. They were horrified—and no doubt filled with righteous indignation—to hear how he had renounced Christianity and become a servant of the Devil. Here's how it happened:

One day, nineteen years earlier, Pierre's flock of sheep had been frightened by a severe storm. Pierre braved hail, rain, lightning, and thunder to search for them, for they were his only means of livelihood. Just as he despaired of ever seeing them again, he met three strangely sinister horsemen.

"What is the matter?" asked one, who appeared to be their leader. "Are you lost?"

"No," replied Pierre, "but my sheep are. I'd give anything to find them—they're all I have."

The head horseman smiled and exchanged a glance with his fellows. "Well now," he said in his oily voice, "that should be easy to arrange."

"It should?" said Pierre eagerly. "Tell me how! What must I do?"

An old woodcut showing a young man making a pact with the Devil.

"Nothing very much," said the horseman casually. "Simply promise to serve me—I am not a very exacting master—and arrange to meet me here precisely one week from now."

Pierre was so excited at the prospect of getting his sheep back that he agreed without a further thought. And sure enough, before the week was out, his sheep returned, safe and sound.

Filled with gratitude, Pierre hurried to keep his appointment with the horseman a week later.

"Kneel down," said the horseman in a terrible voice, when Pierre came up to him.

Pierre felt suddenly frightened, but he was more afraid to disobey than to do what he was told. Trembling, he knelt at the horseman's feet.

"You must vow to serve me," the horseman said, "and you must renounce all other gods. Swear!"

Pierre's voice shook and his body broke out in goose bumps; he had been brought up a good Christian and he went to church every Sunday faithfully. But he swore.

"Renounce the saints," ordered the horseman, and Pierre did. Before the horseman let him go, he had renounced the Virgin Mary, all of Christianity, his own baptism—and had promised never again to set foot inside a church.

"Remember," boomed the terrible one, "I will protect and guard your sheep as long as you obey me. Never again will they stray or fall ill if you obey. Will you? Will you obey me?"

"I will," whispered Pierre, for without his sheep, he would starve.

"Kiss my left hand," said the demon—for such, of course, Pierre now knew him to be—"and rise."

Still trembling, Pierre went home.

It was a long time before Pierre recovered from his terrible experiences. But when two years went by without his seeing the horseman again, he began to wonder if it would really hurt for him to go back to church. True, nothing bad had happened to his sheep—but maybe if he guarded them extra carefully himself, they would continue to be safe. Defiantly, Pierre went back to church.

Nothing happened. He went again, and again, and once more, and nothing happened still. His sheep stayed fat and healthy; their wool was thick and brought a good price, and Pierre soon allowed the memory of that long ago night to fade into a distant nightmare.

Nine years passed, and all was well. Safe, prosperous years for Pierre—until he met Michel Verdun.

"Pierre Burgot," said Michel, sidling up to him one day, "you have forgotten your lord."

"Wh-what?" stammered Pierre, for a minute thinking he must mean the Lord he worshiped every week at church. "Of course I haven't."

"No, your lord, your lord whom you swore to obey," snarled Michel. "You have been going to church in violation of your promise to him."

The distant nightmare came back full force, and Pierre felt himself trapped by the demon once more.

"Your lord wants to see you again," whispered Michel. "You must come with me tonight to do him homage."

Pierre heard one of his lambs bleat as if frightened, and said that he would go.

That night Michel led him to an open space in the middle of a thick wood, where there were many people dancing in the flickering light of torches. Michel ordered Pierre to strip and then covered him with an ointment which he said his "lord" had given him. To his horror, Pierre felt his own hands and feet turn slowly to paws, his human face to a wolfish muzzle, and his skin to a hairy pelt. As he watched, Michel smeared himself with the ointment too and, like Pierre, changed into a wolf.

That first night all the two werewolves did was run around the countryside—but the next time, when Pierre was used to wolf-shape and could manage his four legs, Michel led him in an attack on a seven-year-old boy. The child screamed and Pierre was still human enough to run quickly to the open space in the wood and change himself back to a man.

Later victims, though, did not always scream, and gradually Pierre got used to being a savage wolf whenever Michel commanded. They killed an old woman and a little girl (they ate her, but Pierre had a stomachache afterward); then they killed a woman and drank her blood. Their next victim was a goat, and then another little girl.

Demons and witches sometimes rode to the sabbat on wolves.

At last one night Michel misjudged his victim—he picked a lusty, well-armed traveler, who wounded him and then followed his bloody trail home. By the time the man arrived Michel had turned back to human shape—but the traveler recognized him for what he was, because he bore the same wound as a man that he had received as a wolf.

It was not long before Pierre, too, was caught, and both men, along with a third werewolf, were tried. Despite his earlier attempts to reform, Pierre, like the others, was condemned to death and executed.

Gilles Garnier, tried in 1573, like Pierre Burgot admitted to trafficking with the Devil and changing his God-given human shape to that of a wolf. He was a hermit and had lived alone for many years in a place called Dôle in the south of France. Most people stayed away from him because of his extreme ugliness—certainly added to by the heavy eyebrows which grew in a straight line across his forehead and met over his nose. Eventually, though, Gilles Garnier married, and took his wife to live with him in his lonely forest cottage. The couple kept to themselves the way Garnier had in his bachelor days; they had no friends and seldom spoke to anyone. No one bothered them, and they bothered no one.

But then, in 1572, several neighbor children were attacked one after the other—first a ten-year-old girl, and then another, and then a young boy, and then another. Most of the peasants blamed a wolf for the attacks—but a few said, "No; it is Garnier. See how he keeps to himself and how his brows grow across his nose; it is Garnier."

One thing led to another, and the rumors grew so much that Garnier and his wife were arrested. At his trial, in January, 1573, he admitted to attacking the children—and, more horrifying still, he also admitted to having killed them for food. It was decided that, like Pierre Burgot, Garnier had been led astray by the Devil, and that the Devil had given him a shapeshifting ointment. Garnier himself seemed to believe this—even though someone testified that he'd seen him in *human* shape preparing to eat one of his victims.

Gilles Garnier was sentenced to death and burned at the stake for his sorcery. But this was no deterrent, apparently, to other werewolves, for within ten years came the attack on Benedict Bidel's sister, soon followed by the incident of Jeanne Perrin and Clauda Gaillard.

Real wolves were just as much of a threat throughout this period as werewolves. There were reports, especially during long cold winters, of children being carried off by starving wolves and whole villages being terrorized by hungry packs. These animals were so frightening, and religious beliefs were so full of folklore and superstition, that many people still believed all these wolves to be creatures of the Devil.

As the 1600's approached, though, and the religious climate became a little more tolerant, people began considering other factors. They were still afraid of the Devil and his servants—but they began to take a closer look at those whom they suspected of dealing with the Devil, and they began also to change their own approach to such individuals.

In 1598, for example, came the case of Jacques Roulet.

Jacques Roulet was a beggar who, if possible, was even more ugly-looking than Gilles Garnier. His clothes were ragged, his nails uncared for; his body was covered with lice, his beard long and untrimmed, his hair matted. He was arrested one day in a lonely rural spot near the mutilated body of a boy of around fifteen. The peasants who had happened on this shocking sight said they had seen three wolves near the body. Two had run away, but one had stayed near the body so long that the peasants were able to chase it—only to lose it in the surrounding underbrush. The next living creature the peasants saw was Roulet. Since he was covered with blood, even under his nails, and acted guilty, he seemed to them a likely suspect.

The local magistrate inquired into Roulet's background and discovered that he had two friends, Jean and Julien, who shared his poverty with him and who accompanied him from village to village seeking alms. When questioned Roulet confessed—and confessed—and confessed. Yes, he had killed the boy; yes, he was a werewolf, so were Jean and Julien—they were the other two wolves the peasants had seen, only they had been able to run away faster. Yes, he had killed many others while in wolf-shape, including a bailiff (sort of a deputy sheriff) who was tough to eat. Yes, he had been to the witches' sabbat and, yes, he had a special ointment; it had been given to him by his parents, who had dedicated him to the Devil long ago.

One wonders how much of this confession came from Roulet himself and how much was suggested to him by his captors. Some say his confession was confused and garbled; others say his speech was so poor he sounded more like an animal than a person. Nevertheless, Roulet was eventually sentenced to death but—and this is the first sign that people's ideas about werewolves were changing—his sentence was appealed and then changed to two years' imprisonment in an insane asylum.

A new element—or a nearly new one—had entered the picture: that of mental illness as a cause of, or even a major explanation for, werewolfery.

The next big French werewolf case, as far as we know, came a few years later, in 1603. It was also, apparently, the last of the really big ones. As in Garnier's case, suspicion started when peasant children began disappearing in one district. One after the other they vanished, especially in small villages and country settlements in the district of Landes. Some parents tried to comfort each other by saying their children were only lost and would soon be found—but others would not be consoled. "It is wolves," they said, "and when a wolf carries off a child, the child is never seen again."

A few people hinted at an even worse explanation: werewolves. After all, the creatures were becoming quite common and some people had even seen a suspiciously large wolf—perhaps even with human eyes—slinking around in the area.

When young Marguerite Poirier, thirteen, was attacked and later told her story, there was little doubt that the attacker was, indeed, a

A hungry werewolf attacking a victim. From a sixteenth-century woodcut.

werewolf. What's more, there was little doubt about who the culprit was.

Marguerite spent her days looking after her father's cattle, as did many of the girls in her village of St. Paul. She had been jumped on, she said, one moonlit night, by a wolflike animal, which had run off—but, worse than that, she had also been attacked in full daylight by the creature. That time she had seen that the beast's fur was red, and that it much resembled a large dog—or a wolf. It had come so close this time, the terrified girl said, that it had ripped her skirt with its ugly teeth.

As word of this got out, a young boy named Jean Grenier, who was about Marguerite's age, began telling people that it was he who had attacked her—in wolf-shape. He had, everyone immediately noticed, red hair—long and messy at that. He also had large teeth, so ill-formed that some of them stuck out even when his mouth was closed. He had huge strong hands, and clawlike nails—and he hadn't been in the neighborhood very long, for he was a runaway from another village. No one in St. Paul knew much about him, except that he was poor and tattered and thin, and that he occasionally did odd jobs or hung around annoying the village girls.

After Marguerite had told her story, other girls came forth with theirs. Jeanne Gaboriaut, who worked for someone who had also employed Jean, said he had bothered her by paying her forward compliments and saying that he would one day marry her. To discourage this, she had asked who his father was and he had replied coarsely that he was the illegitimate son of a priest—a very shocking thing to say to a properly religious French girl in those days. When Jeanne commented on how dirty Jean was he told her—so she said —that he was dirty because he often wore a wolf's skin. "I go with nine others every Monday, every Friday, and every Saturday, as the moon wanes; we hunt—especially for children, who are delicious. But sometimes we only get dogs."

Naturally, no one could say something like that and not immediately be suspected of having carried off—perhaps even killed and eaten—the missing children. Accordingly, Jean was questioned by the authorities. He told them about the wolfskin also, saying that someone called the "Lord of the Forest" had given skins and shape-shifting ointment to both him and a neighbor. Jean said he had been introduced to the Lord of the Forest by this neighbor and that the Lord had made a mark on his leg with a little knife. He was now his servant, and was forbidden by him to cut his left thumbnail—which was, the authorities quickly noticed, hideously long, thick, and mis-shapen.

The authorities decided to try to trace Jean's background. It was not long before they discovered that he was not a priest's son, as he had told Jeanne, but a laborer's, and that he had been missing from home for three months. "My father," Jean said at one point during his long trial, "rubbed me with the ointment three times himself; he knows about it; he helped me. Once he even went with me and we killed and ate a girl in a white dress." Jean also said, however, that he had run away from home because his father had beaten him and because he detested him.

Whether it was because his story often contradicted itself, or because he was quite young, or because he was clearly of less than normal intelligence, something in Jean Grenier seemed to arouse the sympathy of the men who heard his case. They were thorough in their investigations, and when the trial finally ended in September, 1603, the president of the court said that Jean's belief that he was a wolf (only one other person—Marguerite—had claimed to have seen him in wolf-shape) was the result of a hallucination. This hallucination had led him to murder and, yes, perhaps also to cannibalism.

No one, however, could help Jean; no one knew how in those days. All they could do was send him to a monastery where, it was hoped, the kindness of the monks and the mercy of God would be able to shelter him from his own delusions. But it was not to be; Jean, arriving at the monastery, insisted on walking on four legs like a wolf. Although he eventually stopped doing that, shortly before he died—at the young age of twenty—he said he still longed to eat raw human flesh. The Lord of the Forest, he said, had visited him twice.

VI

LOGICAL EXPLANATIONS...?

THE IDEA OF WEREWOLFERY's being the result of insanity was not a completely new one, though it had never been very popular, and it was rarely, if ever, seriously considered in Europe before Grenier's time. But from his case on, people gradually began to think of werewolfery more as a mental disorder than as an example of Devil-ridden sorcery.

It is possible, of course, that werewolfery—or lycanthropy, as the mental disorder is technically called—was at least partially caused by drugs. Many of the drugs used as ingredients in "magic" shapeshifting ointments are capable of causing hallucinations, even in normal people. Given a good dose of belladonna, a person can be certain he sees things that are not really there. Henbane, another popular ingredient in shapeshifting ointments, can also cause hallucinations. After using it, many witches were convinced that they could fly. Hemlock, also an ingredient, causes extreme weakness of muscles. Aconite causes a tingling sensation. Opium, everyone knows, can cause hallucinations. Under the influence of such powerful drugs—some of which don't even have to be swallowed to be effective—it is no wonder that many people believed themselves to be wolves—especially if there was a werewolf scare on in the neighborhood or if someone else suggested to them that they had changed shape.

But what of werewolves who didn't use drugs? What about lycanthropy?

Lycanthropy—the disease in which people think they are wolves—has been recognized as a mental disorder for several centuries. Although much of the research on it is inconclusive, people have come up with some interesting ideas and observations. Lycanthropes, for example, do not necessarily believe that they shapeshift back and forth from human to wolf-shape; they often believe they are *real* wolves. Remember the "werewolf" who insisted that his fur grew on the inside of his skin? Many a lycanthrope has given the same explanation when asked why, if he is a wolf, he still looks exactly like a person.

Various cures for lycanthropy were tried back in the sixteenth century as more and more people began to recognize it as a legitimate disease. Few of the cures did much good in the long run, although some may have had a temporarily soothing effect—cures such as bathing the patient in pure water and/or milk, giving him various soothing drugs, and letting him sleep.

Lycanthropy may have physical as well as psychological causes. One sixteenth-century remedy—feeding the patient wholesome food—indicates that people have long been aware of the possible connection between werewolfery and nutritional imbalances. One sad lycanthrope in France, for example, despaired because his friends and family did not seem to recognize that he was a wolf. He touched his mouth and claimed it was a wolf's mouth; he tried to point out the long hairs which he believed covered his "paws." He asked to be allowed to run into the woods so he could be shot there as a wolf might be—and he begged pitifully for raw meat to eat.

Many lycanthropes have expressed similar animal cravings for

Nutritional imbalances and mental illness caused many "werewolf" attacks.
Engraving by fifteenth-century artist Lucas Cranach.

meat. Some have even been out-and-out cannibals. Around 1850, in
a small woodcutting village in Austria, a beggar named Swiatek appeared regularly Sunday after Sunday, asking for alms. Unlike most
other beggars, he sold little ornaments in return for the charity

given him, so he was well thought of; besides, he had a long white beard and looked respectable.

One Sunday a man named Mazur invited Swiatek to have dinner with his large family, and Swiatek accepted eagerly. He was especially taken with one of Mazur's children, a girl of about nine. He gave her a ring with a glass stone, which she proudly took outside to show her friends. Swiatek seemed especially interested when Mazur told him the little girl was not actually his own child but an orphan whom he had taken in.

When the child came home again, Swiatek told her that if she went to a certain tree, turned around three times, bowed to the moon, and said the word "Zabof!" she would find more rings like the one he had given her.

The little girl ran off eagerly to try her luck, and Swiatek left soon afterward. The girl was never seen again.

Some time later several small boys, on their way home from school, missed one of their number, a boy named Peter. Finally they spotted him, talking to a strange man. He seemed deep in conversation, so they went on without him. That was the last glimpse anyone had of Peter.

Next, a servant girl disappeared from the neighborhood, and then a boy, sent to get water from the village well.

The people of the village began to be frightened. These events seemed like the attacks of wolves they had heard about elsewhere in the country—but still, there seemed something unusually odd, something sinister and mysterious about these particular attacks. Still, the villagers reasoned, perhaps that was simply because it was happening in their own village, where they had always felt comfortably safe.

That spring, the local innkeeper discovered that some of his ducks were gone. For some reason, he immediately suspected the beggar, Swiatek—perhaps because he was poor and might need the ducks for food. But the innkeeper needed them, too, to feed his guests—so off he marched to Swiatek's cottage.

As he drew near he smelled meat cooking—but when he arrived, Swiatek hastily hid something under his clothes. The innkeeper, thinking it might be one of his missing ducks, grabbed Swiatek and wrestled with him till the hidden object rolled out into view.

It was not a duck. It was the head of a young girl.

Swiatek, as one might imagine, was arrested shortly thereafter, as was his whole family. His cottage was thoroughly searched, and sure enough, the rest of the young girl was found, divided into sections and prepared like animal meat for the oven.

Swiatek confessed that he had killed and eaten six people—with his family—but his own children said that they had eaten more than six. Sure enough, a great many articles of clothing, no doubt belonging to various people not in Swiatek's household, were found in his cottage.

Finally Swiatek explained how he had acquired his cannibalistic tastes. A few years earlier, a tavern had burned down near where he lived. At the time, he was starving. While poking about in the ruins of the tavern, he had found a partly roasted human being. Since he was so desperately hungry, he ate it—and since that day he had craved human flesh above all other food.

Swiatek was imprisoned to await sentencing. But the world will never know how fairly or unfairly he might have been treated, for the poor man hanged himself the first night he was in jail.

In 1598—over two hundred and fifty years earlier—a French tailor was sentenced to death for tastes similar to Swiatek's. According to testimony at his trial, he had killed a number of children in order to butcher and eat them as most people would beef or mutton. As proof of this bizarre taste in meat, the authorities produced a barrel of human bones they had found in the tailor's house.

Horrible as these stories are, they show how a physical plus a mental illness may have been what motivated many werewolves. Suppose a person did have a dietary deficiency which gave him an abnormal craving for meat. Suppose—as was often the case in the Middle Ages—fresh meat was hard to come by; it was either unavailable or it was so old and poorly preserved it had to be thoroughly cooked with rich spicy sauces to be edible. Sauces could destroy the true meat flavor, and besides, the poor couldn't afford them. (It was usually poor peasants who were accused of being werewolves, or who believed themselves to be.) Human meat, on the other hand, was readily available and could be had freshly killed. There was no need for sauces.

Nowadays most people can easily satisfy a meat craving by going to the nearest supermarket or restaurant. But four or five hundred years ago it was not so easy. Who knows how many werewolves there might be today if meat were scarce! Cannibalism isn't all that unusual. People have become cannibals in times of famine. Even as recently as World War II, when the Russian city of Leningrad was besieged for nearly two and a half years, there were reports of cannibalism. Couple that with the religious superstitions of early Christianity—and the terror people had of wolves—and you have a logical explanation for werewolfery that has nothing to do with magical shapeshifting.

People have suggested other logical explanations for lycanthropy. One—closely related to the drug idea—involves dreams. If a mentally unbalanced person frequently dreamed that he was a wolf, might he not someday become convinced that he really was one?

Another explanation is rabies, a horrible disease of animals and man which is nearly always fatal and which wolves transmit more easily than, say, dogs. One symptom of rabies is an inability to swallow, which leads to and intensifies a great thirst on the part of the victim. (Remember that extreme thirst has been considered a symptom of werewolfery.) Another rabies symptom is strange, often wolfishly aggressive behavior. Rabies occurs all over the world, and has frequently been most prevalent late in the winter and early in the spring. (Werewolves, remember, were said to be most active in the month of February.) A final symptom of rabies is paralysis—which makes one think of Benedict Bidel and Perrenette Gandillon. Suppose Perrenette had rabies and, shortly before becoming crippled by paralysis, attacked Benedict's sister? Suppose, as Benedict defended her, she bit him? Paralysis might then have overtaken her —and Benedict himself might have died of rabies, not of a wound made by a werewolf's claws or a devilish knife.

There are also little-known and rare diseases which could have contributed to the spread of the werewolf superstition. There is, for example, porphyria, an inherited disease in which people have discolored teeth and are so sensitive to light that if they go into the sun they develop ugly blisters. People with porphyria are often horribly deformed—as many werewolves were said to be. The disease, rare though it was, usually ran in families when it appeared—and frequently was shared by brothers and sisters of the same parents. This might explain werewolf families like the Gandillons.

Then there is also another rare, also inherited, disease called hypertrichosis, whose victims are unusually hairy all over their bodies. Naturally the more hair a person has the more animallike he appears, especially to those people who don't know that such a thing can be caused by a disease.

Werewolf stories spread because of crime, too. Some people have used other people's fears of werewolves to their own advantage. You've already heard of the Byzantine thief who tricked the innkeeper into believing he was a werewolf so he could steal his cloak. In sixteenth-century France, since there was already widespread fear of werewolves, poachers—those who hunted on other people's property—pretended to be wolves in order to avoid being caught and punished as men. Cults of "leopard men," "panther men," and

This man may have been a victim of hypertrichosis, a disease characterized by unusual hairiness all over the body.

"lion men" in various African countries have used similar cover-up techniques to commit serious crimes, including murder. But perhaps the most famous criminal were-animals of all were the Nordic berserkers—from whose actions comes the expression "going berserk."

Berserkers, who were around before Christianity was widespread, were men dressed in bearskins (sometimes wolfskins) who worked themselves into a frenzy of excitement and then fiercely attacked others. Some people said they were insane or possessed by the Devil. But others said they used their frenzy and their animal disguise to make their victims tremble and bend to their will. A warrior berserker was invincible in one of his "fits," so the legends say; no sword could penetrate him (perhaps no sword could penetrate the armorlike hide he wore over his very human and very vulnerable body).

Berserkers were best known, though, for their cruel attacks on villages and lonely farms. Knowing how much they were feared, they would attack with confidence and arrogantly challenge individual farmers to a fight. If a farmer lost, everything he owned—including his wife—went to the berserkers. The same thing happened if he refused to fight, so the farmer had no choice but to accept the unfair challenge, one which he was likely to lose. A poor peasant, cowering in terror before a frenzied berserker attacker, might not realize that the creature who confronted him was really more man than beast. Perhaps all he could recognize as human were the creature's reddened eyes, burning out of his animal pelt with blood lust and cruelty. . . .

VII

NOT QUITE WEREWOLVES

THERE WERE—still are—beliefs in werewolflike creatures all over the world. Many such creatures, however, don't shift into wolf-shape. The loup garou of Haiti, for example (and his cousin in Canada), unlike his French counterpart, can change himself into almost anything he wants—even a tree. Like the European werewolf, though, a wound he gets in his changed shape will always show up on his human body when he changes back.

Here are some other werewolflike creatures:

India: the *rakshasa* or *raghosh;* attacks and eats people. Like the Haitian loup garou it can change its shape to anything it wants. In human shape, it is huge and has red or yellow hair (most people in India have black hair)—lots of it.

Persia: a creature like the Indian rakshasa; preys on travelers and often disguises itself by turning into a camel or other harmless animal to which a traveler—especially a stranded one—might be attracted.

Iceland: the *hamrammr;* a person whose shape shifts into that of whatever animal it eats. Not only that, but he acquires the strength of that animal and adds it to his own; the more animals a hamrammr eats, the stronger he grows.

Kenya, Africa (Kikuyu tribe): the *ilimu;* a people-eating shape-shifter. The only thing is, this creature is not a man to begin with; it is an animal who can change its shape into a man's!

South America: the *kanima;* an evil soul or spirit in jaguar-shape, often sent to kill an unpunished murderer.

Then there are the wolf-related creatures who are definitely wolves or wolflike, but who aren't, strictly speaking, *were*wolves. The *lubins* or *lupins* of Normandy, France, looked like wolves, but they used human speech (although no human could understand a word they said). They weren't fierce like most werewolves—in fact most of them were so shy that they ran away from anyone who came near them. Instead of attacking the living, these timid beasts dug up graves and ate dead bodies.

Another werewolf-related creature in France was the being who sometimes led packs of werewolves or who guided individual ones —somewhat like poor Jean Grenier's Lord of the Forest or Pierre Burgot's evil horseman. This leader was often believed to be the Devil or at least a lesser demon. He was a humanlike creature but he could use wolf-shape if he wished.

One of the most famous werewolflike creatures in France was the Wild Beast of Gévaudan. No one really knew what kind of animal the Beast was, or if it really was an animal. Some people said it was a wolf suffering from rabies. Some said it was a hyena which had somehow strayed to France; others thought it was a panther. There were people who insisted it was a cross between a lion and a tiger or a wolf and another animal, and there were others who maintained it was a warlock—a male witch—who had changed his shape. After it was dead, its skull was found to be larger than that of the largest wolf seen locally; scholars now say the Beast itself, judging from the

The Wild Beast of Gévaudan, which is believed to have devoured more than a hundred inhabitants of that French village in 1764–65.

size of its skull, must have been as large as any wolf now known.

Whatever it was, the Wild Beast was terrifying and had most of the good people of Gévaudan quaking during the year it stalked their district. Its record was astounding: more than one hundred people killed and eaten in 1764–65.

The bravest of Gévaudan's people went out after the Beast. But even stout-hearted fighting men found the creature impossible to capture or kill. Anyone who managed to conquer his fear of the Beast's cruelly sharp teeth and strong tail (which it used like a club) still had to overcome his disgust at the nauseating stench it emitted. And anyone who could ignore the stench and approach it had to contend with the Beast's ability to leap up into the air to dizzying heights. Time after time people tried to kill the Beast and failed. A few succeeded in freeing some of its victims; an eleven-year-old boy managed to save four younger children from its clutches. But—while all Gévaudan shook with fear—month after month went by without anyone's being able to stop the terrifying creature.

Eventually one of the king's soldiers came to Gévaudan. "I will kill the Beast," he said, and of course no one believed him. But this mysterious soldier, who was known simply as Monsieur Antoine, went out by himself one day (as far as anyone knows), killed the Beast, and quietly went back to wherever he'd come from. No one knew why or how Monsieur Antoine managed to succeed where so many others had failed—but no one in Gévaudan asked very many questions, they were so glad to be free of the Beast at last.

The *wawkalak* of Russia was another kind of werewolf entirely. He was a person who had made the Devil so angry that he had been changed into a wolf as punishment. The wawkalak, however, never did anything harmful and was often so tame that his family and friends tried to protect him. But wawkalaks were doomed to wander, so they could not stay long among those who loved them.

Closer to the werewolf was the Slavic *vlkodlak*, sometimes a drunkard, sometimes a child born with teeth, or just a person changed into a wolf by the magic powers of another. If that was the case, the vlkodlak would usually stay meekly near his own village, waiting till the prankster who had changed him into a wolf changed him back. There were vlkodlaks, though, who were harmful. Back in the 1200's it was believed that they caused eclipses by eating the moon or the sun. In those days people were afraid of eclipses, and the local peasants used to rush outside with drums and noisemakers

China was one of the places where it was believed that solar eclipses were caused by werewolflike creatures. Here, a mandarin tries to save the sun from being eaten.

to drive the vlkodlak away and save the "threatened" heavenly body. Vlkodlaks could change into creatures other than wolves, and the harmful ones attacked farm animals at night, or strangled people.

One of the goriest werewolf-related stories of all time is about a vlkodlak. He didn't shift his shape, but he was as bloodthirsty as any four-legged werewolf.

This vlkodlak had nine beautiful daughters, all old enough to be married. None of them had married, though, and their father eventually got tired of feeding so many mouths. After thinking the whole thing over, he hit on a way to solve his problem.

"I must go into the forest," he told his daughters, "to cut wood for the winter. Bring me my meals when it is time."

The girls agreed, and the evil vlkodlak went chuckling off into the forest.

At lunchtime his eldest daughter came to him with a delicious meal for which he thanked her politely. When he had finished eating, he said, "Come, I want to show you something."

Trustingly, the girl followed her father to a deep, freshly-dug pit. "Why, Father," she asked, with some surprise, remembering he had said he was going to cut wood, "why have you dug this pit?"

The vlkodlak smiled evilly. "I have dug it for us, my dear, when we die—as you shall do right now." Ignoring the girl's pitiful screams, he killed her and pushed her into the pit.

Back he went to the place where he had been pretending to cut wood. At dinnertime his next oldest daughter brought him another delicious meal. "Come," he said, when he had finished eating and smacking his lips with enjoyment, "let me show you what I have made for us." He took her to the pit, too, and treated her as he had her sister.

And one by one, he killed all his daughters in the same way—until he came to the youngest, who was also the most beautiful.

Now she was as wise as she was beautiful, so she was on her guard against him. Instead of walking straight up to him trustingly as her sisters had done, she hid herself at a safe distance and watched him for a while. And it was well she did, for her worst fears about her missing sisters were immediately confirmed. There in the clearing where he sat, her father had built a huge fire, and on it he was roasting parts of his dead daughters!

The youngest daughter controlled her grief and her fear and

came out of her hiding place. She crept off to one side of the clearing and called to her father.

The vlkodlak came eagerly, rubbing his hands together.

"Where," asked the girl as she handed him his dinner, "are my dear sisters? They have not been home for many days, Father, and I am worried about them."

"Oh, they are piling wood up for me in the valley," said the vlkodlak. He added craftily, "Come with me and I will show you."

The girl followed him obediently, but she kept her wits about her.

At the edge of the pit, the vlkodlak could hardly control his pride in the evil deeds he had done. Chortling, he explained to her what he had done to her sisters. "You too," he said, reaching for her, "you too must follow."

The wise girl pretended to submit, but she moved away just enough so the vlkodlak could not reach her. "Turn your head for a minute," she said, "for if I am to die, some poor woman in the village could get some use out of my dress. Turn your head while I take it off."

Impatiently the vlkodlak turned—and the moment he did, his clever daughter gave him a great push which sent him tumbling into the pit with the bodies of his other eight daughters.

But the wise girl ran the second she saw him fall, for she feared he might be able to climb out easily; the pit was not too deep. Again, she had guessed right, for within a few minutes she heard the vlkodlak running fast after her. Soon he was gaining on her, soon she could hear his wheezing breath and feel the vibrations caused by his heavy feet.

Just as the vlkodlak was about to grab her, the clever girl held her handkerchief out behind her. The vlkodlak was so angry at catching it instead of his daughter that he ripped the dainty scrap to shreds before resuming the chase, thus letting the girl gain slightly on him. When he was about to catch her again, the girl threw her apron at him, and that allowed her even a little more time in which to get ahead.

Finally, panting for breath, the girl came to a hayfield and just as her father came out of the forest after her, she plunged into a pile of hay. The vlkodlak tore round and round the field, searching for her and howling with rage, but though he hunted for hours, he could not find her. At last, exhausted, he slunk off into the forest.

The next day the king, out hunting, crossed the hayfield and found the beautiful and intelligent girl. He took her home to his palace and in time fell in love with her and married her. The new queen made only one demand of her husband: that no beggar should ever be allowed into the palace. It seemed an odd request from one so kind as she had shown herself to be, but the king agreed.

Years passed, and the king and queen were very happy together. Their peaceful lives were rarely interrupted by anything more alarming than the momentary crying of one or the other of their two tiny sons.

Then one dark day a new servant, forgetting the rules, let a ragged beggar into the palace. Slyly, the beggar sneaked out of the kitchen where he had been brought to be fed and crept stealthily up the stairs to the nursery. Cruelly he killed the two baby princes who slept there, and then went out into the forest where he laughed and rolled on the ground with glee. "I have paid her back," he cackled; "I have paid her back well for outsmarting me!" For, of course, the beggar was none other than the evil vlkodlak, the young queen's father.

There was weeping and wailing in the palace when the murders were discovered. The queen turned away from the bloody cradles in silent grief, sure she knew who the killer was. But the king, half mad with sorrow, misunderstood her actions. "You must have done it," he shouted, pointing a shaking finger at his pale and frightened wife.

"You were last with them, and see, you do not weep for them."
While the servants watched helplessly, the bereaved father tied the
dead princes together with a piece of rope, hung the rope around
the queen's neck, and drove her out of the palace.

Overcome with unhappiness, the queen walked along the road
that led to the forest. Great tears spilled down her cheeks, but she
still could not cry out loud. What would be the good? Nothing could
bring her babies back, and no one could explain her innocence to
the king—indeed, she was certain that no one could restore his wits.

But then she passed by a tiny cottage that huddled on the edge of
the forest. A bent-over, ancient hermit sat on a stone in the cottage's little tangled garden and said softly, as she passed, "Good
day, Majesty. What fine boys you have."

At that moment—just as she turned her head to look at the hermit—the queen felt a tugging at her neck. "Mother, put me down,"
came a familiar baby-voice, and a younger baby-voice whimpered.

The astonished queen took the rope from her neck and her weeping changed to laughter as she saw that her little sons were restored
to her, alive and unhurt.

"Go back to your husband," said the old hermit, smiling. "Go
back; all will be as before."

The grateful queen flung her arms around the hermit's neck to
thank him and then hurried back to the palace.

The king was waiting for her, his mind as sound as ever and his
heart sorry for betraying her in his grief. The royal family lived happily ever after from that day on, and never again were troubled by
the evil vlkodlak.

To return to the shapeshifters: the were-creatures of non-Euro-
pean countries—the werelions and weretigers, werefoxes and were-
buffalo—behaved very much the way werewolves did. In Africa, for
example, most shapeshifters chose hyena, leopard, or lion-shape,

Shapeshifting was not always entirely successful. Some were-creatures could only change partway into animals.

since these were the most common fierce animals in that part of the world. There is one story of a man who claimed, in 1947, to be a werehippopotamus—but, despite the fact that he rooted about in someone's garden, supposedly in hippo-shape, no one believed him!

In Nyasaland, though, an old man was believed, at least somewhat, when he confessed to murdering a number of people while in the shape of a lion. He said he periodically felt himself changing and that when he did, he was overcome by the impulse to kill.

Among many African peoples, certain sorcerers were said to have the power to change into were-beasts. In Ethiopia, Morocco, and as far south as Tanzania, blacksmiths, most of whom were considered sorcerers, had this special power. They were called *boudas*, and usually changed into hyenas. Like werewolves, boudas wounded in animal-shape kept the same wound in human shape. They often drank an herb mixture to bring on transformation, and some, like Navajo werewolves, robbed graves. Unlike werewolves, though, these creatures frequently wore, as animals, some ornament they had on as humans. Sometimes this was the way they were identified when caught. In Upper Volta, for example, when a certain young female hyena was shot, she was found to be wearing earrings. The earrings, it was discovered, belonged to the daughter, recently declared missing, of a local chief. Piece by piece the story came out. The girl had been the chief's favorite daughter, so he had arranged to have her marry before her older sisters. But her sisters were jealous and worked out a clever means of murdering her. First they had the girl locked up and tormented until she, driven insane, began to behave like an animal. Then the older sisters gave out that she had become a werehyena. Once they were sure they were believed, they had the girl murdered, and carefully placed the gold earrings she always wore into the ears of a female hyena. When the hyena was shot—and they probably made pretty sure it was—all the older girls had to do was say, "Look, see our poor sister who has turned into an animal. What a sad thing that is—but, poor thing, she is probably better off dead."

There are also many African folk stories about werelions. One werelion who lived near the Zambezi River was even provided with a safe and comfortable den by his faithful wife. She brought him food every day while he was in lion-shape, and guarded the mixture he had to drink in order to change back. No one was allowed to lean a gun against the walls of this werelion's den, because he was afraid of the smell of gunpowder. He used to hunt in his own village, and it was said that even his wife was afraid he might someday attack her. Perhaps that is why she took such good care of him!

In some places werelions were thought to be lion bodies housing the souls of dead chiefs. One such creature prowled around a hunters' camp, sniffing at the newly dressed meat. A hunter tried to shame him into going away by saying that he couldn't have been much of a chief if he had to nose around other people's food. Another hunter tried the same argument, but more politely. But it was only when a third dipped some of the meat into poison that the werelion-chief went away!

People in other countries—Malaysia, for example, and India—where the tiger is the most feared and respected animal, told about weretigers. In some parts of India people didn't believe in shape-shifting, but thought there were those who could send their human souls into the bodies of tigers. (Some occultists today in this country explain the shapeshifting of European werewolves in somewhat the same way.) In India, also, the connection between were-creatures and drugs or insanity was recognized early. Some drug-ridden or mentally ill people, it was noticed, went into the jungles of India at night and rode on the backs of tigers. Though they were called weretigers, most people who observed their strange daytime behavior felt there was something more than magic or bedevilment afoot.

From Malaysia, however, comes the story of a weretiger named Haji Ali who, as far as is known anyway, was neither mentally ill nor on drugs.

Haji Ali was a trader who had two sons. He settled in a small village and soon married a girl named Patimah. (Perhaps his sons' mother had died—or perhaps he had more than one wife.) Patimah's father and mother were pleased with the match, for they were poor and Haji Ali was rich. Imagine their anger, then, when after three days of marriage Patimah came home in tears in the middle of the night and said she never wanted to see Haji Ali again. Ah, but imagine their horror when she explained why not: Haji Ali, she said, had not spent a night at home since the wedding. On this very night, Patimah had decided to wait up for him. "I went to the door when I heard him coming," she told her parents between sobs, "and I opened it, and there was not my husband but a tiger—

111

a tiger who changed into a man, into Haji Ali, before my eyes!"

Naturally after hearing that, Patimah's parents told her she needn't ever go back to Haji Ali, rich or no!

Word of this ghastly event spread quickly around the village. Soon no one would talk to either Haji Ali or his sons. Then one night a tiger—or so everyone thought—killed the Headman's water buffalo. As was usual in such cases, the Headman built a trap in which a gun was rigged to go off when the trap was sprung.

The next day, the trap had been sprung all right, and the gun fired, but there was no dead tiger lying there. Instead, a bloody trail led from the trap into the jungle. The Headman and some of the villagers followed the trail deep into the jungle until at last they came to Haji Ali's house—where the trail ended.

"No," said Haji Ali's sons to the Headman, "no, our father cannot see you, he is ill." The blood, they claimed, was a goat's blood.

"We *must* see him, nonetheless," said the Headman. "It is vital— we must see him, if only for a minute. He need not even talk."

But the sons continued to refuse and the Headman, who was a peaceable individual, didn't want to barge in uninvited. Beckoning to his followers, he turned away and went back through the jungle to his own house.

Not long after that, Haji Ali moved away. Someone from the village claimed to have seen him some time later, when he himself was on a trip—and he said that Haji Ali now walked with a limp. A limp, people speculated, very like one that might result from a gunshot wound. . . .

Marriage between a human being and a were-creature is a frequent theme in both African and Asian folklore. Usually, though, the normal situation is reversed: instead of a person changing to an animal, in most marriage stories it is an animal who changes into a person—frequently so he can eat his spouse once the marriage ceremony is over.

A *pre-Columbian Inca painting of a tiger-man.*

In one story, from Nyasaland, the little brother of a beautiful young bride follows the newly married couple home, convinced that the groom is really a hyena. When they reach the groom's village, the couple allows the little boy to stay; after all, he has come all that way and it would be cruel to send such a small child home at night all alone. The boy prepares his bed outside the young couple's hut that night, but he does not let himself fall asleep, for he is still convinced that there is something evil going on. And he is right—for later, after the village has grown still, a band of hyenas circles around the hut, singing about how they are going to eat the bride as soon as she has been fattened up. The little boy realizes to his horror that not only is his sister's husband a hyena but all the villagers are also. He and his still-unsuspecting sister are smack in the middle of a village of hyena-people!

In the morning, the haggard boy tells his sister what he has seen, but she doesn't believe him. She thinks that he must have had a bad dream and that he is trying to lure her home with him so he can play with her as he did before her marriage. He pleads with her to allow him to prove that what he has told her is true. "Let me wake you up tonight when they sing," he begs.

"But how?" she asks. "You cannot come inside with us, my husband will never allow it. And if he"—here she suppresses a giggle—"if he is a hyena too you cannot come inside to wake me, for he might eat you up."

The boy tells his sister to tie a string to her toe before she goes to sleep and to let him keep the other end outside with him. "I will pull it," he says, "when the hyenas come, and that will wake you."

The young bride, although annoyed, decides to humor her small brother. "Maybe," she thinks, "he will find out he is wrong and go away and leave me alone."

That night when the hyenas gather around the hut—for of course they do—the little boy tugs on the string and it is a very contrite older sister who admits that he is right. "What shall we do?" she wails. "Oh, what shall we do?"

But the brother has thought of that, too. Borrowing his brother-in-law's tools, he spends the day making a strange large bowl. That night, when the hyenas come, he puts his sister into it and while she looks on amazed he sings a magic song. The bowl-shaped vehicle rises smoothly into the sky and carries the two of them back safely to their own village.

In China and Japan, there are similar—although not so sinister—marriage stories. Here, the were-animal is usually a fox, and usually female. Any fox, it was said in China, who lived to the age of five hundred could shift into human shape with no trouble at all—although in some stories he (or she) had to put a human skull over his head and bow to the Big Dipper first. In another version of this legend, it was only necessary for a female werefox to be fifty years old

A pottery figure of a Mexican god who was thought to assume the shapes of many animals. Here he is shown as a werejaguar.

before she could change into a woman. At the age of one hundred, she turned into a sorceress who had a kind of second sight enabling her to know what was happening as far away as one thousand miles. Finally, at the ripe old age of one thousand, these were-creatures went to heaven—but more as living beings than as the souls of dead people.

There were many ways to recognize werefoxes disguised in human shape, if one knew what to look for. Some turned back into foxes whenever they slept—and others always kept their tails on, no matter what. A werefox, when made to look into a still pond while in human shape, would always reflect as a fox. A werefox wounded in human shape always turned instantly back into an animal. One could always change a werefox back by cutting off its tail, reciting certain spells or charms, arguing with it if it was in the shape of a scholar, or by killing it.

Sometimes, though, people were deceived for years by werefoxes, especially those who changed into beautiful human women in order to get men to marry them. It was quite a shock for a man to discover, upon the death of his wife, that the woman he loved had really been only a fox the whole time!

Men who found out their wives were really foxes were often, as one might expect, furiously angry. But sometimes love was stronger than anger. An old Japanese story tells of Ono who, after years of looking, finally found the woman of his dreams. He married her and loved her more and more every day. After a while, his wife gave birth to a fine son, and at the same time, his dog gave birth to a puppy. Much to Ono's distress, the puppy and the woman never liked each other. In fact, the situation became so bad between them by the time the puppy grew up that the wife asked Ono to kill it. "I can't do that," he said. "How can you ask me to kill my dog?"

The wife had nothing to say to that, and things went on as before. But finally one day the dog attacked her. She was so frightened that she turned into her true shape—yes, that of a fox—and ran away.

But Ono, shocked as he was, couldn't bear to lose her. He begged her to return, and told her that he didn't care if she was a fox or not. And so the couple resumed their marriage on a new basis: the wife roamed the woods as a fox by day, and returned every night, as a loving wife, to her husband.

There's also the story of the upper-class girl in India who married a tiger who was in human shape. One day she annoyed her husband by talking too much. "Be quiet," he ordered when all else failed, "or I will show you my true shape."

Well, that made the girl quiet, all right—at least on whatever subject she'd been chattering about. But she was so curious that she begged her husband to show her his shape. He refused; she went on begging—and so, to shut her up again, he turned into a tiger before her astonished eyes.

She was not so happy then, poor girl, but she had no choice but to go on living with him; it would not have been proper for her to leave her husband. She stayed on, a quiet wife now—until one day she gave birth to not the son she had hoped for but a bouncing baby tiger cub!

After that, she decided to ignore what was proper and go home to her father's house. Her relatives were full of sympathy and took her in. "Of course you may stay," they told her and she, relieved, settled down in her new life.

But some of her cousins and brothers stole out the next night, found her weretiger husband and killed him. "See what we have done," they told her proudly the next morning. "We have killed him; he will never bother you or any other girl again."

But strange is the power of were-creatures. The Indian girl, instead of rejoicing at the death of her weretiger husband, went quietly outside and planted a bush in his memory!

VIII

A WORD ABOUT MODERN WEREWOLVES

SOME PEOPLE THINK werewolfery is such an old superstition that no one believes in it anymore. It is certainly true that there are not many people nowadays who believe that human beings can shape-shift into wolves or other animals—but despite that, there have been reports of werewolves in modern times.

These reports have often come from isolated parts of the world, where wolves are still seen in large numbers. Actually, wolves are still more prevalent than many people realize. A Turkish village suffered from them as recently as the winter of 1971, when hungry packs ate eighteen sheep dogs in two days. In 1963 a pack of wolves was seen in France, and in the early sixties there were reports of wolves in Italy, Portugal, Spain, and Poland. In North America, though they are in some danger of extinction, there were nonetheless close to fifty thousand wolves in 1972. Perhaps because there are still so many wolves—and because people still fear them—were-wolf stories have persisted well into the twentieth century. For example:

1923, Greenwich Village, New York City: When a group of friends was experimenting with the *I Ching*, a book of Chinese magic, and practicing some of the rituals it describes, one participant, a woman, accidentally "tossed" a hexagram which had the power to cause shapeshifting. (In following the *I Ching* in order to do magic, you toss certain small sticks into the air. As they land they form six-sided figures—hexagrams—which are believed to have special powers.) After a while the woman, in a sort of trance, claimed to be wearing a fur coat. (She was not.) Then she said she was running through snow (she was really indoors), which she said she could smell as clearly as any dog. Finally she crouched on the floor and began baying and yelping as a hunting dog or wolf might do. When one of her companions tried to bring her out of her trance, she snarled at him viciously and tried to bite. . . .

1925, France, near the German border: A policeman killed a young boy who had been teasing him unmercifully. It seems the policeman believed that animals with human faces were tormenting him, and the boy had preyed on his belief. The boy, claimed the policeman, was able to shift his shape into that of various animals. *Everyone else in the village agreed that this was so.* . . .

1930, France: A farmer, whose house was full of sorcerers' equipment (herbs, magic stones, dried salamanders), and who made love potions for the local girls, was seriously believed by his neighbors to turn into a wolf at night. . . .

1932, Wales: A professor on vacation found what he thought to be a dog's skull in the lake near a cottage he had rented. He took it back to the cottage, planning to examine it carefully, for it seemed unusually large. But that night when he was out, his wife heard a scratching sound at the door—and, looking out the window, saw a terrible creature, which stared rudely back at her. It seemed part

Despite scholarly probes into the origins of werewolfery, some attacks remain unexplained—even in modern times.

human and part wolf—its face was a wolf's but its paws grasped like hands and its eyes had a human look.

The beast kept snuffling around the house till the professor came home. Later that night the beast returned and the professor and a neighbor, who had been watching with him, both saw it. They agreed with the wife that it had the face of a wolf and the eyes of a man.

The two men chased the werewolflike creature to the lake, where it mysteriously disappeared. And the next morning the professor threw the strange skull back into the water. The beast with the human eyes troubled them no more. . . .

1946, U.S.A.: People on a Navajo Indian reservation were convinced that year that one of their number was a werewolf, that he robbed graves and killed and ate women. . . .

1949, Rome: One summer night police heard wolflike howls coming from a clump of bushes. There was a full moon. The police advanced cautiously, not knowing quite what to expect. Finally they saw the creature responsible for the howls—a man, digging furiously in the mud with his hands as an animal might. They took him to a hospital, where he explained that for the past few years every time the moon was full, he had felt these strange uncontrollable urges. . . .

Truth? Superstition? Madness? Illusion?
You decide!

SELECTED BIBLIOGRAPHY

UNFORTUNATELY some of the most complete books about werewolves are very old and out of print—some are as many as one hundred years old. Others are long, complicated, and hard to read. Recently, however, there has been a rebirth of interest in werewolves—so in a few years it may be easier to find material. In the meantime, here is a list of some of the more readable and available books and stories.

BOOKS

Aylesworth, Thomas G., *Werewolves and Other Monsters*. New York, Addison-Wesley, 1972.
———, *Monsters from the Movies*. Philadelphia and New York, Lippincott, 1972.
Cohen, Daniel, *A Natural History of Unnatural Things*. New York, McCall, 1971.
Douglas, Drake, *Horror*. Macmillan, New York, 1966.
Leach, Maria, ed., *Standard Dictionary of Folklore, Mythology and Legend*, 2 vols. New York, Funk and Wagnalls, 1949.
MacCulloch, John Abbot, ed., *The Mythology of All Races*. New York, Cooper Square Publishers, 1932.

Ross, Marilyn, *Barnabas, Quentin, and the Body Snatchers*. New York, Paperback Library, 1971.

———, *Barnabas, Quentin, and the Nightmare Assassin*. New York, Paperback Library, 1970.

STORIES

Bierce, Ambrose, "The Boarded Window"
———, "The Eyes of the Panther"
Blackwood, Algernon, "Running Wolf"
Kipling, Rudyard, "The Mark of the Beast"
de Maupassant, Guy, "The Wolf"
Sayers, Dorothy L., "The Cyprian Cat"
Walpole, Hugh, "Tarnhelm"

INDEX

ABOUT THE AUTHOR

Nancy Garden, born in Boston, Massachusetts, spent her childhood in various parts of New England, and was graduated from the Columbia [University] School of Dramatic Arts, later receiving her master's degree from Columbia Teachers College. She has been an actress, stage-lighting designer, teacher, and editor, but is mainly devoted to writing. Her published books for young people include two novels, WHAT HAPPENED IN MARSTON and THE LONERS, and nonfiction, including a companion book to WEREWOLVES, called VAMPIRES. Ms. Garden lived in New York City for several years, but now shares a home in the country with a friend and two golden retriever puppies, and spends most of her spare time gardening.